METAMORPHOSIS

METAMORPHOSIS

The Gift of a Life Lived Twice

CRISTINA FONTANA, RN

Dedication

To my parents, Pier Franco and Diana: Thank you for your love and guidance. Though our time together was brief, your influence continues to shape who I am.

To my children, Gabriela, Tomás, and Alex: You are my greatest inspiration. Through my journey, I hope to teach you the power of resilience and remind you that life always offers us the chance to write and rewrite our stories.

To my husband, Daniel: You are my anchor and my closest friend. Thank you for walking beside me through every twist in the path and for helping build a life filled with love and meaning.

To my sister, Pepe: You have been a quiet force of strength in my life. Thank you for inspiring me to strive for excellence and become the best version of myself.

To anyone who feels lost after the death of a loved one: May this book offer you hope, the courage to begin again, and the strength to reclaim your purpose beyond the pain.

PUBLISHING

Soulfully Aligned Publishing

Table Of Contents

Dedication iii

Foreword ix

Introduction...xii

Chapter 1 1
Finding Strength in The Storm 1

Chapter 2...19
What Gives Our Life Meaning?...................................19

Chapter 3...40
A Flower Beginning to Bloom....................................40

Chapter 4...59
The Beauty in What Remains 59

Chapter 5...77
Believe You Can and You're Halfway There................77

Chapter 6...98
Creating Ripples of Hope...98

Chapter 7...118
Rising Above the Peaks 118

Chapter 8...142
The Healing Connection 142

Chapter 9...157

How Would They Want Me to Live?...........157

Conclusion 198

Acknowledgments......................................201

Thank You 205

Author Bio 207

About The Publisher 210

Soulfully Aligned Publishing.......................210

Foreword

Can you imagine walking into a hospital to donate a kidney—not to a friend or family member, but to a complete stranger? No expectation of thanks, no connection to the recipient. Just a quiet, selfless decision to give someone a chance at life?

That's what Cristina Fontana did.

Her choice was not a sudden impulse. It came after a lifetime of learning how to endure and transform.

As a teenager in Venezuela, Cristina watched her father, the anchor of her family, fade away from cancer. That loss upended her world but also planted in her the conviction to help others. She began medical school, determined to care for patients like him. But when political and economic turmoil made Venezuela unsafe, Cristina and her husband left everything behind—her studies, their home, their family—to start over in Indiana with two young children and little more than determination.

She rebuilt her career in healthcare, first as a radiation technologist for cancer patients, and then as a nurse. Along the way, she chose to donate her kidney to a stranger. And then she turned that experience into a vocation, becoming a nurse coordinator to guide other living donors through their journeys.

This book tells that story—not just the medical details of surgery, but the deeper journey of loss, reinvention, and purpose. Cristina writes with clarity and honesty, offering a rare window into what it means to give, to grieve, to begin again—and to find unexpected meaning in the middle of it all.

Metamorphosis: The Gift of a Life Lived Twice is more than a personal story. It's a reminder that transformation often starts with uncertainty. That healing sometimes begins when we reach beyond ourselves. And that giving—real, wholehearted giving—has a way of making us whole in return.

It's an honor to introduce this book, and to celebrate Cristina Fontana—not only as a donor, but as a colleague, a caregiver, and an inspiration.

John Powelson, MD

Kidney donor surgeon

June 2025

Introduction

You may already know my phobia: butterflies. Yes, those magical insects most people associate with beauty, transformation, and freedom have always frightened me. For as long as I can remember, I've felt an instinctive aversion to them, as if they carried an unspoken message I couldn't yet understand. Ironically, butterflies have since become a symbol I deeply identify with, a metaphor for my life.

Life has a curious way of unfolding, doesn't it? What once disturbed me now serves as a profound teacher.

Recently, I began working with Emily, a mindset coach who guided me through deep self-reflection and growth. During our sessions, butterflies kept showing up in our conversations, in my dreams, in everyday moments. At first, I resisted. Then, one day, it clicked. I began to see them differently. Their life cycle, in all its detail, mirrored something within me. What I had once feared was now illuminating my path.

After one particularly moving session, I emailed her and shared the title I had just discovered for this book: *Metamorphosis: The Gift of a Life Lived Twice*. Her response was full of encouragement:

"Cristina! That is so beautiful! Thank you for sharing. I'm so glad you were inspired this week. A huge accomplishment to move out of that freeze state and start writing. Proud of you! So many more breakthroughs ahead! – Emily"

In the months working with her, I came to understand that butterflies don't simply flutter into being. They begin as caterpillars, humble, grounded creatures. At a certain point, the caterpillar retreats into its cocoon, a process that may seem passive but is anything but. Inside, it breaks down into a cellular soup and transforms in total darkness. Fewer than five percent survive the transformation.

And here's the remarkable part: if you try to help a butterfly by easing its struggle out of the cocoon, you will rob it of its ability to fly. It is the very struggle that strengthens its wings.

This truth hit me deeply. How often do we wish for an easier path? How many times had I, unknowingly, been inside one of these cocoons? Each struggle, each moment of darkness, had been building my wings.

My earliest cocoon formed when I was fourteen, after my father died of cancer. His loss shattered my world. He had been my anchor, the one who made me feel safe. Without him, I was adrift. Maybe you know that feeling. Perhaps you've picked up this book because you've experienced your own devastating loss, a parent, a partner, someone who grounded you.

When grief wraps around us like a cocoon, it disorients. Up becomes down. Forward feels impossible. But here's what I've learned: the cocoon is not the end. It is a beginning. It is a place of transformation.

At the time, I couldn't have imagined that life would take me from the streets of Venezuela to the mountains I'd climb around the world. I couldn't have foreseen that the girl paralyzed by grief would go on to build a career in healthcare, donate a kidney to a stranger, and dedicate her life to helping others find their strength. Every milestone was born in struggle, in those dark, dissolving spaces.

Looking back, I see the pattern. Each chapter of my life demanded deep transformation. Each one taught me that struggle is not the enemy, it is the metamorphosis.

If you're grieving now, know this: you are not alone. The cocoon you feel trapped in is not your ending. It is your chrysalis. While you can't always control what happens, you *can* choose how you respond. You can rebuild. You can live again. You can live twice.

That is what this book is about: the gift of living twice.

This is the story of how I found hope in loss, purpose in pain, and the courage to rewrite my life. I invite you to walk with me through this journey, across continents and memories, valleys and mountaintops.

As I write this now, butterflies no longer terrify me. They remind me of what it means to endure, to transform, and to emerge stronger.

This could be your beginning, too. Your wings are already forming. Let this be your time to rise.

Figure 1: my parents

Chapter 1

Finding Strength in The Storm

"You never know how strong you are until being strong is your only choice."

~ Bob Marley

The morning of November 6, 1982, is engraved into my memory. It was the day everything changed, the day my world cracked open and would never fit together the same way again.

Around 6:00 am, the sharp ring of the phone sliced through the stillness. I wasn't fully awake yet, but the sound made my chest tighten. The air felt heavy, as if it were trying to tell me something before my mind could catch up. I lay frozen in bed, staring at the ceiling. My sister, Margherita—Pepe, as I call her—was sleeping next to me. I could hear voices whispering down the hall. My aunt, *Tía Betty*, spoke softly, but with a trembling edge in her voice *"I'm so sorry, Fru,"* she said, using my mom's nickname. *"I'll let the girls know."*

Even before I heard the rest, my heart already knew the truth: my father was gone. The world seemed to stop at that moment, as if time itself had frozen. My chest tightened, my breath grew short, and tears streamed down my face uncontrollably. I pressed my face into my pillow, trying to quiet the sobs, but the pain was overwhelming. My chest felt hollow as if my heart had been scooped out of place. I was only fourteen years old, and yet, I felt like I had aged a hundred years in a single moment, burdened with grief I didn't know how to hold.

I still remember the walk from the parking lot of Policlinica Metropolitana, the local hospital, to the silver elevator that took us to his room. Every day after school, we went there, searching for something normal. Our books lay scattered on the sofa bed next to him as we did our homework, the constant hum of the machine draining fluid from his lungs fading into the background. Some days, friends picked us up and took us to their homes for dinner before we came back to repeat it all again the next day. On other days, we just went home with Tia Betty, my aunt.

But today was different. Today was the last time I'd make that walk. I felt scared, yet somehow relieved. The endless days of worry, hospital visits, and watching him slip away were done. But then what? How would life be without him? Would I ever see him again? Those questions felt too big to grasp, too heavy to process. I was angry that I never got the chance to say goodbye, and time ran out before I even knew it was running out. I have very few memories from those days; my mind is shielding me, trying to keep that pain away. Even now, 43 years later as I write this, that pain still brings tears.

This time, his hospital room was silent; no beeping, no machines, just an emptiness that filled the space. Patty, my best friend, and her mom were there.

I remember her mom gently tying a handkerchief around his mouth to close it. The image stays with me. I didn't want to see him like that. I didn't want to touch him, and I didn't want to acknowledge that this was real. But I had to. His skin felt cold, not like the warmth of his hand I had held so many times before. It was like rubber, lifeless and unfamiliar. I kept thinking this was a nightmare I could wake up from, but it wasn't.

And just like that, everything changed.

Growing up in Caracas, Venezuela, our family was small but close. There were just the five of us: my parents, my older sister, me, and our playful blonde Cocker Spaniel, Judy. We didn't have many relatives nearby, but our home still felt cozy, a place where love was always present.

My parents adored each other. They were a perfect match, a blend of elegance and strength, each bringing their unique heritage and charm to our family. My mom, Diana Marsh, was an American with a graceful style that came from her upbringing in a wealthy mining family in Caracas. At 5'8", with chestnut curls falling past her shoulders and her signature cherry-red lipstick, she radiated class and sophistication everywhere. Her dresses and skirts highlighted her slender figure, and she carried herself with confidence. My dad, Pier Franco Fontana, was an Italian civil engineer with a strong build, olive-green eyes, and black wavy hair that made him seem warm and approachable. Standing at about 5'10", his kindness was as striking as his smile, which could light up any room. He had moved to Venezuela in the 1960s, seeking opportunity and a way to support his family back in Italy. Together, they were the kind of couple everyone could see was meant to be.

Our life was comfortable, even privileged. Together, they built a beautiful life that seemed unshakable from the outside.

The neighborhood I called home as a kid was *Urbanization Santa Rosa de Lima.* It's situated on the outskirts of the capital city. We lived in a 12-story building, on the fourth floor, in apartment 4-A. The building was named *Residencias Valle Alto* and stood in a private cul-de-sac with only two buildings.

A security guard watched the gate, controlling who came in. If visitors showed up, he'd call us before letting them through. Our home was on a hill facing *El Ávila,* and the view was something I'll never forget. Big, sunlit windows and tall balcony doors opened up to the green slopes of *El Ávila,* the mountain that wrapped around the valley of Caracas. I loved sitting on the balcony, staring out at the city. To me, *El Ávila* symbolized strength, stability, and protection; qualities I saw in my dad too.

But life has a strange way of unraveling in the moments you least expect.

The weeks before my dad died were hard. Each day bringing a new heartbreak, hurting more than the last. His illness moved fast, like a thief taking him away piece by piece. At first, it was little stuff he'd forget where his glasses were or the names of people we knew well. Then it got worse. He'd lose whole conversations. One evening, something happened that stuck with me forever.

We were on the balcony, our usual spot before dinner, watching the sunset behind the mountains. It was quiet, just me and him. Most nights, we'd chat about school, homework, or joke about little things. But that night felt off. My dad turned to me; his olive-green eyes clouded with confusion.

"Who are you?" he asked.

I stopped breathing and froze for a second. "Dad, it's me," I said, my voice shaky. A nervous laugh escaping my lips as I tried to make sense of what he meant, but his blank face told me it wasn't a joke.

My stomach twisted. Panic hit me hard, and I ran to find my mom.

"Mom! Dad just asked who I am! What's going on?" I cried, my voice cracking from fear.

She was in the kitchen, her hands shaking as she put down a dish. She pulled me into a hug, her voice unsteady. "The cancer is in his brain now," she said softly, her words thick with sadness. "He's not himself anymore."

I held onto her tight, my tears soaking her shirt, as I tried to make sense of something that felt so senseless. My dad, the one who'd always been my rock, my guide, my protector, didn't know who I was.

This wasn't the first time I thought I might lose him. When I was nine, my dad had surgery at MD Anderson in Houston, Texas, to remove the cancer in his kidney. My mother, my sister, and I went to Houston too, spending the summer with our cousins, Susan and Sharon. At first, being in Houston felt like an adventure, especially since we were young and didn't fully understand how serious things were. We played by the pool, stayed up late watching movies, and laughed until our stomachs hurt. But beneath all that fun, there was a constant ache. I missed my dad so deeply it hurt, and every night, as I lay in bed and prayed, I wondered if I would ever see him again.

He survived that surgery, but the shadow of cancer hung over our family for the next five years. Doctor visits, treatments, and constant worry became our new normal. Then, one day, the news we dreaded came. Now, five years later, it felt like that same fear had returned, only this time, it was different. I was older now, and the reality of losing him felt more real, more final.

The day he died, my mom held the funeral in the afternoon. No autopsy, no need to drag out the pain any longer. It felt like a strange dream I desperately wanted to wake up from. The funeral home was filled with school friends and strangers, their voices low as they offered condolences. I stood beside my dad's casket, staring at the man inside. His once warm and lively face was now pale and still, a stranger in familiar clothing. At one point, I heard a faint gurgling noise coming from the casket, and I froze, a wave of panic rising in my chest.

"Is he still alive?" I whispered to my mom.

"No," she assured me, her eyes red from crying. That moment haunted me for years; in ways I couldn't fully understand.

In the weeks and months that followed, the house felt empty without Dad. Every corner seemed to echo with his absence, the chair where he used to sit and drink his whiskey or help me with math homework, the faint scent of his cologne that lingered in the hallway, the silence that replaced the sound of his laughter. It felt like time had stopped for us, but the world outside kept moving, like it didn't notice we were hurting.

I worried about Mom. She tried to be strong for us, but I could see how much she was struggling. I could see the weight of her grief when she thought no one was looking. I heard quiet sobs from her room, and she would lock herself in her bathroom and smoke. We were all lost, trying to figure out how to live without him.

I didn't know how to process my grief. It felt like a storm raging inside me with no outlet. Then, one day, I picked up a pen and started writing. It was like finding a valve to release the pressure building up inside me. Journaling became my refuge, a place where I could pour out all the emotions I couldn't say aloud. I wrote about how much I missed him, about the anger I felt at the unfairness of it all, about how lost I felt without him. Writing didn't fix anything, but it gave me a way to release the pain I was holding inside. It was like opening a window in a room filled with smoke, letting in just enough air to breathe.

During this time, school became my sanctuary, my anchor, a place where life felt predictable, even if only for a few hours a day. *Mater Salvatoris,* the all-girls Catholic school Marg and I attended, was a place of order and routine. It sat on a hill, surrounded by tall mango trees, its green gates opening to reveal a world that felt far removed from the chaos of my grief. The air was always filled with the sweet scent of ripe mangoes, and the sound of girls' laughter echoed through the corridors, a stark contrast to the silence that now filled our home. Inside, everything was neat and structured. We wore crisp white blouses and navy-blue pleated skirts, with polished blue moccasins. The classrooms were simple yet inviting, with clean white walls, wooden desks, and a picture of the Virgin Mary on the wall, always watching over us. A dark green chalkboard took up almost an entire wall, and every classroom had light blue double doors with windows letting in streams of sunlight.

One of my favorite subjects was English, taught by Miss Hellen. My proficiency in English came from my mother, a fact which drew envy from my peers. Miss Hellen was a bit heavy and wore olive-green eyeshadow with bold dark red lipstick. Her wrinkled skin showed her years, and her short hair stood out for a woman back then. Still, she had a kind heart, though I didn't see it fully at the time.

One day, in English class, I learned a lesson that stuck with me for years. While Miss Hellen wrote on the chalkboard, I mimicked her, exaggerating her moves to make my classmates laugh. They giggled, and I felt clever, until the room went silent. I turned and saw *Madre Rodriguez,* the head nun, in the doorway, her sharp eyes stare sternly on me.

"Señorita Fontana, come to my office," she said, her voice firm.

"Go on, go on," Miss Hellen said, her wide eyes unsure about the situation.

My stomach sank. I followed Madre Rodriguez, my heart racing. In her office, she scolded me and warned she might expel me. I could hardly speak.

"I'm sorry," I managed to say, my voice shaky and low.

"It won't happen again," I mumbled, staring at the floor as tears dripped onto my polished moccasins.

I cried, realizing how foolish I had been. It hit me then—I'd disrespected someone who only wanted to teach me. I felt ashamed, and the weight of my actions pressed down on me. That moment taught me about respect and owning up to mistakes, lessons that shaped me more than I knew then. Looking back, those school struggles—like this one—built the strength I'd need for life's challenges. It was there I learned to get back up after every fall.

I was more rebellious than my sister, always pushing boundaries and making mistakes. Each mistake taught me something. Every failure, every disappointment was molding me into someone stronger. That grit became part of who I am.

At home, everything felt different. The kitchen, once warm and filled with the aromas of home-cooked meals and family dinners, turned into a place of convenience instead of connection. My mom stopped cooking altogether. We had maids to prepare meals and clean, but it was never the same. Soon, our kitchen was filled with processed foods, chips, cookies, soda, and canned goods. Junk food became the easiest fix in a house where grief drained any energy to care about what we ate.

I turned to food for comfort, filling the emptiness with whatever was at hand. I gained weight, and with it came a creeping insecurity. I barely recognized myself, and my self-esteem slipped further with each passing day. But food wasn't my only escape route, movement was, too. Outside of school, I found comfort in physical activities and prayer. I started jogging with my friend Ana Maria, our feet pounding the pavement in sync, each step lifting me away from the heaviness at home. I also joined a local gym. Exercise gave me a sense of control when nothing else felt certain. I played volleyball at school and swam whenever I could. Movement became my therapy, a way to release all the grief my heart carried.

One thing I loved most about Catholic school was attending Mass on Fridays. The familiar prayers, the hymns, and the way our voices echoed through the chapel felt like a warm blanket around me. In my pain, I turned to prayer and singing as outlets, even though a part of me was angry at God. Still, I summoned faith to pray every night. Mom, Pepe, and I began going to weekend Mass regularly, searching for something—maybe peace, maybe answers to what took dad away from us. Music became a need, speaking to me in ways I couldn't always put into words. Even now, after all these years, I can still recall the melodies and words of many of those school songs. Alongside my journaling and movement activities, music turned into a practice I treasured, a way to process what felt too heavy to bear alone.

Years later, I heard Tim McGraw's song *Live Like You Were Dying,* and it moved me deeply. The lyrics tell of a man who, after facing his own mortality, decides to truly live by taking risks, loving deeply, and cherishing every chance life offered. It made me think of my dad and everything he never got to do. He never saw us grow up, never retired, and never traveled the world with my mom. His life was cut short, leaving so much undone. If you know the song, listen to it now.

That song reminds me of the promise I made to myself after he died: to live fully, take chances, and never hold back. My dad didn't get to *live like he was dying*, but I can choose to live like that for him.

Loss reshapes us in ways we don't always see right away. It breaks us down, forces us to find new footing, and asks for strength we never knew we had. But over time, those hard, painful moments become the very medicine we need, teaching us to keep going, to care more, to endure, and to move forward even when the weight of grief still lingers. What feels too hard to handle today might one day be the reason you stand taller, love deeper, and live with more purpose.

Realizing how fragile life is changes how you see everything. It alters the choices you make, the risks you take, and the love you give.

Grief can feel like being wrapped in a cocoon of sorrow so tight that moving on may seem impossible. Yet even in that darkness, transformation can be found.

I didn't realize it at the time, but every tear I shed, every song I sang, and every word I wrote in my journal was part of my metamorphosis. I wasn't the same person after my dad died. The pain softened me in some ways and made me stronger in others. Like a caterpillar in its cocoon, I let go of parts of my old self, making room for something new, even if I couldn't yet see what that would be.

Figure 2: El Ávila view from our home

Figure 3: Mater Salvatoris school, singing during school mass

Chapter 2

What Gives Our Life Meaning?

"In three words I can sum up everything I've learned about life: it goes on." ~ Robert Frost

I can still see it clearly, as if it were yesterday. Every summer from the time I was two or three years old, my family traveled to Italy to visit our relatives at a very special place: Via Vitaliani 30. In the beautiful town of Porto Azzurro, what was once a modest fisherman's house became our treasured family home, echoing with memories of the past. It is a place of warm sun, laughter, and quiet sadness. A reminder of a mother's love, her grit, and the sacrifices made for the sake of her family.

19

That mother was Ermelinda Fontana, my great-grandmother. In the late 19th century, she left everything behind to cross the ocean to Venezuela, settling in a small town called Carache in the state of Trujillo. She made the journey with her husband, who was from Capoliveri, a neighboring town on the island of Elba. When she discovered his infidelity, she did the unthinkable: she left him and returned to Elba alone, bringing her seven children with her.

Back in Elba, her family judged her harshly. As punishment for leaving her husband, she was given the farthest house in town, a humble fisherman's house, isolated from the rest. Yet what was meant to symbolize disgrace became a place of strength. She built a life for her children, including my grandfather, Edoardo Fontana, and turned that simple house into a warm and loving home. In this quiet corner of Porto Azzurro, our family's story truly began.

Elba is a small island in the Mediterranean, just ten kilometers off the coast of Piombino in the Tuscan Archipelago. Covering 86 square miles, it is Italy's third-largest island after Sicily and Sardinia.

Elba offers more than its association with Napoleon's exile in 1814. Accessible by ferry or a small airport with limited connections, the island captivates visitors with its volcanic landscapes and breathtaking views from Monte Capanne, its highest peak at 3,343 feet.

Divided into eight municipalities, Elba is home to about 30,000 residents. Portoferraio is the largest town, but our family's heart belongs to Porto Azzurro, once known as Porto Longone. With its Spanish influence, colorful buildings, and lively charm, Porto Azzurro feels timeless. Life there revolves around Piazza Matteotti, where the marina fills with yachts in summer and fishing boats in winter. Along the waterfront, where charming restaurants now stand, sits our ochre-colored family home. Its warm tone blends seamlessly into the pastel hues of the town, a quiet but enduring testament to where we came from.

For some, family is as strong and secure as the walls that hold a house together. For others, it is fragile, like a glass vase shattered into pieces. For us, it was both. Once broken, a vase seems impossible to repair, but with patience, each fragment can be carefully glued back into place. The scars remain, but they tell a story of survival. The fisherman's house, once a mark of disgrace, stands today as a symbol of fortitude, transformation, and love.

One memory that remains vivid in my mind is a quiet conversation I once overheard between my parents. My father asked my mother to keep his memory alive and to take us to Elba so my sister and I would never forget where we came from. I watched my mother cry as she reassured him, she would honor his wish.

And she did.

Elba became a constant in our lives, a place where we reconnected with our Italian family, built friendships, and, for a brief time, let grief melt into joy. It became a sanctuary where sorrow softened, replaced by the simple pleasures of laughter, new friendships, and the smell of Zia Mina's freshly cooked meals.

I still remember Saturday mornings at Il Mercato, waking up with the excitement of a child in a candy store. I would throw on my fuchsia swimsuit, a blue polka-dot sundress, and flip-flops before racing to the kitchen.

"Andiamo!" I'd shout, loud enough for the neighbors to hear.

"Un momento," Zia Mina would reply, always calm, always elegant. She would carefully place her small leather purse over her arm, dab on her signature Chanel perfume, and brush through her snowy white hair. Even in her late seventies, my great-aunt, my grandfather Edoardo's sister was effortlessly graceful. She always wore a blue dress, pearls, and strappy leather sandals. Her pink lipstick often ended up on her teeth rather than her lips, but I was mesmerized by the ritual of her getting ready.

"Ok, andiamo," she'd finally say with a smile as we stepped outside. I would skip ahead, still within reach, until her voice stopped me.

"Attenzione, Cristina!" she would call as a car passed.

Although the market was only a few blocks away, the walk always felt like a journey. When we arrived, I would dart through the stalls, weaving between vendors who greeted me with a warm "Buongiorno!" I knew the market by heart. My favorite booth overflowed with ponytails, hair accessories, hats, and nail polish. The vendors always recognized me.

Meanwhile, Zia Mina moved at her own pace, exchanging greetings and pausing at a stall filled with colorful ceramics. She would admire the handcrafted vases, eventually choosing two adorned with bright lemons, perfect for the sunflowers we had bought that day.

Some of my fondest memories in Elba are from the summer of 1983 and 1984, when I spent my days with my closest friends. Each morning, Aldo would pick me up, and together with my cousin Francesco, we would head to 3 Punte at the end of La Pianotta Beach, a rocky formation divided into three levels—perfect for diving into the crystal-clear water below. Along the way, we would greet neighbors and friends, many of whom had known us since childhood. Their familiar faces added warmth and comfort to the rhythm of summer.

Francesco's parents, Mario and Nicla Porta, were always welcoming. Nicla's sister, Fernanda, had married Giulio Berti, Zia Mina's first cousin. It was during these brief summers in Elba, surrounded by extended family, that life felt whole again. Giulio would even travel to Rome to pick us up, making sure our journey to Elba was smooth and filled with care.

Our group of friends, Aldo, Lucia, Paola, Mauro, Stefania, Valeria, Viviana, Silvia, Laura, and Andrea, became like a second family to me. We spent our mornings at La Pianotta, savoring gelato while sitting on the stone walls across from Andrea's bar, planning how to spend our afternoons. One of my favorite treats was La Coppa Del Nonno, a creamy, coffee-flavored gelato that remains a beloved indulgence.

After long hours under the sun and swimming in the sea, hunger would set in. Zia Mina always had something wonderful waiting for us at home. She had a gift for making every meal feel special. Our plates were filled with tender chicken, sweet peas, and her signature creamy risotto. Each grain of Arborio rice was perfectly cooked, steeped in rich chicken broth, and finished with a generous handful of grated Parmigiano Reggiano. My children still call it "special chicken," and it remains a cherished dish in our family.

Evenings overflowed with music. Lucia, Aldo's sister, and Stefania would strum their guitars, and we all joined in to sing *Il Gatto e La Volpe* by Edoardo Bennato. The warm night air, the echo of our voices rising into the twilight, and the closeness of those friendships made time feel endless, filled with joy and belonging.

For forty-five magical days, that rhythm of connection became my summer. It remains one of the most treasured seasons of my life. In Elba, grief stepped aside for a moment and allowed laughter to take its place. For a brief and beautiful month, happiness returned. Even now, many of those childhood friends remain part of my life. The love we shared during those summers continues to this day. We may have grown older, but when we reunite, it feels as though no time has passed.

Family has always been my foundation. Growing up in Venezuela with Italian and American parents, I often struggled to answer the question, *Where are you from?* The truth is, I felt like I was from everywhere. We sang happy birthday in three languages, celebrated Halloween and Thanksgiving, honored Three Kings' Day as they do in Venezuela, and at Christmas, we gathered around a table filled with *Hallacas*, one of Venezuela's most treasured holiday dishes, rich with flavor, wrapped in banana leaves, and slow-cooked with love.

My friends didn't always understand our customs, but they loved being part of them. Each holiday was a new adventure. One day we'd be carving pumpkins. The next, we were gathered around a Thanksgiving table, savoring a stuffed turkey. At Mater Salvatoris, the small all-girls private school I attended, friendships became like family. There were only sixty girls in my graduating class, if that tells you anything.

At the time, Caracas was home. The breathtaking view of the mountains grounded me, a constant reminder of strength and peace. But there was also Río Chico, our beloved beach house, about two and a half hours from the city, on the other side of the mountains. It was more than just a house; it was my father's dream brought to life, a place where his love touched every detail. The bathroom tiles were imported from Italy. Our mustard-colored boat, *CrisMar*, was named after my sister and me. It was where we escaped the city's chaos. After he passed, it became a sanctuary filled with memories of him.

There were good days and bad days, moments of despair where I clung to old birthday cards and photographs of my father and me. As the years passed, I would return to them often, searching for comfort in his handwriting, in the frozen traces of his voice, and in the memories that helped me feel close to him again.

I often thought about love. Who would I marry? Would I find the kind of love my parents shared? Their relationship had always been my model, something I carried with me, something I longed to experience. My father's favorite song, *'O Sole Mio,* which was also the name of our house in Rio Chico, often played in my mind as I imagined a marriage grounded in deep, enduring love. That melody always brought tears to my eyes. Every Sunday, he would play it at full volume on his old record player, filling the house with music and memory.

My connection to music ran deeper than I realized. On my father's side, through my grandmother Caterina Cherici, our family carries a remarkable lineage. We are related to the legendary Italian composer Giacomo Puccini, known for timeless masterpieces like *La Bohème* and *Madama Butterfly*. His music continues to echo through opera houses around the world, stirring hearts across generations. This connection has always been a quiet source of pride in our family.

My father was born in Lucca, a beautiful city in Tuscany, and spent his early life between Viareggio and Torre del Lago, the very places Puccini once called home. Torre del Lago, in particular, holds special meaning for us. It is where Puccini composed many of his greatest works while overlooking the serene waters of Lago di Massaciuccoli.

I remember the first time I visited Torre del Lago as an adult, accompanied by one of my father's closest friends, Piero Conti. It felt like coming home to a part of myself I hadn't even known was missing. I walked quietly along the edge of the lake where Puccini's house still stands, now a museum. The stillness of the water and the softness of the breeze made time feel suspended. I stood there, imagining my father as a young boy, running through those same streets, unaware of how deeply his roots would later shape my own story.

As a child, I didn't grasp the significance of our connection to Puccini. But after my father's death, I began to feel it in quieter ways, in my love for storytelling, in the tears that rise when I hear opera, and in the way I've always turned to creativity to move through grief.

Hearing Puccini's music now feels like a thread weaving past and present together. I close my eyes and hear my grandmother humming. I see my father laughing with his friends in Viareggio. I feel, in my own life, that I am continuing the story, not only through this book, but in the way I live and love.

Grief never truly leaves us. It lingers, quietly reshaping itself into something we learn to carry. I had to build a new version of my life, one that honored my father's memory without being consumed by his absence. Some days, the weight of that loss felt unbearable. But in time, I came to understand that new beginnings are not only possible, they are often born of love.

In those quiet moments of reflection, I found meaning in the memories, in the stories he left behind, and in the lessons, he had unknowingly prepared me for. The ache remained, but so did his presence, guiding me toward a life of deeper purpose, love, and resilience.

One of the most cherished treasures in my Zionsville home is a simple ceramic vase from one of those visits to the market in Porto Azzurro with my beloved Zia Mina. Every time I see it, I am reminded of my great-grandmother's courage, of the fisherman's house she transformed into a loving home, and of the promise my mother made to keep our family's legacy alive. That vase, though humble, is a symbol of the strength, love, and lineage that continue to anchor us to Elba, to this day.

This love lives on through my children and grandchildren. My son Tomas, inspired by our deep connection to the island, chose to marry in Elba as a way to honor our roots. Now, when my granddaughter Audrey calls me *Nonna*, I feel the quiet joy of passing down these stories and traditions. It's a reminder that the legacy of our family, built on love, resilience, and a promise made long ago, continues.

If there is one thing I have learned through the journey of grief and healing, it's this: we carry those we have lost with us not just in memories but in how we live. Life is never the same after loss, but it can still hold beauty. We honor our loved ones not by clinging to pain, but by embracing life with open hearts. In doing so, we allow love, joy, and new beginnings to shape what comes next. Just as my great-grandmother turned hardship into strength, we too have the power to reshape our story after loss.

I Don't Remember

(A poem for anyone struggling with memories of a loved one)

I don't remember

the scent of your skin

or the sound of your voice

floating through the rooms.

I don't remember

your laughter echoing

or the way your eyes looked

when you were proud or angry.

I don't remember

Christmas mornings,

birthday candles,

or how your arms felt around me.

I don't remember

your smile without a photograph,

your voice without a dream.

I don't remember

the warmth of your hugs,

your kisses on my cheek,

or how you said my name in Italian.

I don't remember

a time when you weren't sick.

But I do remember

the silence you left behind.

I don't remember

how we kept going,

only that we did.

I don't remember

our family

before everything changed.

But I do remember

the abyss that followed.

I don't remember

you being here,

but I always feel

you near.

And even though

my memory fails me,

after all these years,

my love does not.

Because I will carry you

in every breath,

through every year.

And I will love you

beyond distance,

beyond time.

Always and forever.

Figure 4: PortoLongone early 1900s

Figure 5: Porto Azzurro early 1900s

Figure 6: Porto Azzurro today

Figure 7: Via Vitaliani, our Italy home

Figure 8: Our Rio Chico home

Figure 9: Piero Conti in front of Puccini's home

Chapter 3

A Flower Beginning to Bloom

"You cannot swim for new horizons until you dare to lose sight of the shore." ~ *William Faulkner*

As the years passed, I often found myself questioning the purpose of life. I rarely voiced these thoughts, but deep inside, I felt a quiet, persistent pull to help others in ways I had not been able to help my father. The idea of becoming a doctor began to take root. When I shared this with my mother, she didn't fully support it, not because she doubted my ability, but because she understood the sacrifices it would demand. Late nights, exhausting shifts, and a life consumed by responsibility. She gently suggested teaching instead, reminding me how much I loved children. But the idea didn't move me. It didn't stir my soul the way medicine did.

I needed a path that stirred something deeper, one that gave my life purpose. For me, that path was medicine. More specifically, oncology. The decision was not impulsive. I thought about it for a long time. Once I committed, there was no looking back. I applied to medical school and was accepted. The moment I stepped into Escuela de Medicina Luis Razetti in 1987, I felt something settle inside me. I knew I was where I was meant to be.

People often describe medicine as a calling, and for me, it truly was.

One of the greatest comforts during those years was having Ana María by my side. We shared the same passion for medicine, and with her father being a cardiologist, she had his full support. Together, we navigated the intense, sometimes overwhelming world of medical school. We met incredible people, many of whom became lifelong friends, united by a shared commitment to something larger than ourselves.

Escuela de Medicina Luis Razetti is one of the two medical schools at Universidad Central de Venezuela (UCV) in Caracas, the country's most prestigious public university. Its reputation for academic rigor and strong clinical training made it an ideal place for aspiring physicians. Located within the Ciudad Universitaria de Caracas, a UNESCO World Heritage Site, the school offered a unique learning experience. Our days blended classroom instruction with hands-on training at some of the largest hospitals in Caracas, including Hospital Universitario de Caracas. The program shaped generations of Venezuelan doctors, many of whom went on to make a lasting impact both nationally and internationally.

I loved the study of medicine. I was determined to one day find a way to cure cancer. During my time at Luis Razetti, I was honored to receive the Dr. Jose Izquierdo Award for Excellence in Anatomy. This award meant a great deal to me. It set me apart from my peers, and more importantly, it made my mother proud. On weekends, Ana María and I volunteered with the Venezuelan Red Cross and gained practical experience at Padre Machado Oncology Hospital. Those experiences deepened our commitment and gave us a front-row seat to both the fragility and resilience of the human spirit.

In medical school, I formed a close study group with Irving, Pablo, Maria Belén, Elizabeth, Josmar, Andrés, and others. Many of us are still in touch, though life has taken us in different directions. Almost all of them became successful physicians around the world. But among them, one person held a very special place in my heart.

Irving was my first real boyfriend, the first man I brought home. In many ways, he filled the emptiness left by my father's absence. My mother adored him. She admired his kindness, his respectful nature, and the way he treated me, with a love and devotion that felt both comforting and unfamiliar. He gave me something I had been missing, a sense of being cared for in a way that was safe and unconditional.

Irving had a deep love for Def Leppard, a band that remains one of my favorites to this day. The song *Hysteria* still brings back a flood of memories. He drove a white Mustang and loved blasting music with the windows down, the wind rushing through my hair as we sped through the streets, lost in our world. His best friend, Claudio, was dating Ana María, and the four of us often went on double dates, creating moments of carefree joy in the midst of the intense demands of medical school.

Looking back, Irving was more than just a boyfriend. He was the first male figure in my life after losing my father, someone who showed me what it meant to be loved, cherished, and cared for. Our relationship, though it didn't last more than a few years, marked a turning point in my journey toward healing. Through him, I began to understand the kind of love I longed for and the tenderness I deserved.

Grief changes shape, but it never ends. Losing my father at such a young age left a void that no one could truly fill. Over time, though, I discovered that love has the power to soften even the sharpest edges of sorrow. Grief doesn't disappear, and it never follows a straight path. It transforms. It weaves itself into our lives in quiet ways sometimes as a gentle presence, sometimes as an overwhelming tide. In that ebb and flow, I realized something essential: grief is also a reflection of love. The deeper the loss, the deeper the love that once existed.

Irving, my friends, and my studies became the anchors that helped me find my way through that transformation. They reminded me that grief is not only about absence but also about how we carry love forward. I began to understand that grief and love are inseparable. One cannot exist without the other. Rather than letting sorrow define me, I chose to honor my father through the life I lived, the love I gave, and the purpose I pursued. Life kept moving, and with time, so did I, carrying his memory not as a weight, but as a guiding light.

At the same time, my sister was also forging her own path, studying Dentistry at the same university and campus as I was. She often brought her friends home to study, and our house was always filled with the rustle of flipping textbooks, the hum of late-night conversations, and shared frustration over upcoming exams. My mother loved having the house full, and we always had snacks on hand, so our home quickly became a favorite hangout for our friends.

Among them was Daniel, one of my sister's study partners. He was always the life of the group, funny, loud, and full of energy. He loved teasing me, and there was a touch of harmless flirting between us. At the time, though, he had a girlfriend, and I was still with Irving, so our interactions stayed playful and nothing more. I saw him simply as one of my sister's many friends, someone who enjoyed getting under my skin with his jokes and playful remarks.

Something unexpected happened on New Year's Eve of 1989. One of my sister's friends, Ernesto, hosted a party, and both Irving and I were invited. The night was filled with music, dancing, and heavy drinking. Irving, never much of a dancer, sat back while I spent most of the night on the dance floor with Daniel. Caught up in the excitement and the haze of alcohol, I left the party with Daniel, leaving Irving behind. Looking back, I'm ashamed of how it unfolded. That night marked the beginning of my relationship with Daniel.

We dated for just over a year. When I found out I was pregnant, we decided to get married. I felt a deep worry about how this would affect my mother, but I was also excited to become a mother myself. I loved the idea of starting a family, even though I wasn't fully ready for marriage. I was 23. Daniel reminded me of my father in ways I couldn't fully explain. And the truth is, I did love him. With a baby on the way, we did what we believed was right.

Seeing Irving every day in medical school after that was difficult. We didn't speak, and I can only imagine the hurt I caused him. Daniel was nothing like Irving. He was bold, provocative, and had a reputation as a womanizer. Our families disapproved, fearing he would hurt me. Even my sister worried that our relationship would strain her friendship with him. And yet, here we are 34 years later, still married.

I never dreamed of a grand, extravagant wedding. I wanted something simple, intimate, and heartfelt, surrounded by the people who mattered most. A daylight ceremony, where the gentle warmth of the sun touched my skin. Modest floral arrangements with sunflowers. Music we could dance to. A celebration that reflected who we were, not a performance for the sake of tradition. I wanted to stand beside the man I loved and promise a future built on something honest and real.

Still, even with its simplicity, one question haunted me: Who would walk me down the aisle? It was a question I had dreaded since the day my father died. Every little girl pictures that moment, arm in arm with her father, hearing his steady breath beside her, seeing the proud smile he would wear. But he was gone, and the empty space beside me felt like an open wound.

My family suggested my uncle Harry, Tía Betty's husband, thinking a man should take my father's place. But it didn't feel right. The one who had been both mother and father to me, who had carried me through my darkest hours, was my mother. She had shown up every single day. And so, it was her arm I held, steady and strong, as we walked together down the aisle.

There was another tradition I chose to change that day. Taking my husband's last name was expected, but I couldn't let go of Fontana. It wasn't just a name. It was my father's name, his legacy. With no brothers to carry it forward, who would? If I let it go, it would feel like closing a chapter that was never meant to end. Keeping my maiden name was my way of holding onto him and ensuring that Fontana didn't disappear. It was a quiet act of defiance, a tribute to the man who had shaped me, even though he wasn't there to walk me down the aisle.

For my dress, I didn't want to buy something new. It didn't feel necessary when I already had something special, something waiting for a new purpose: my Quinceañera dress. A Quinceañera is a traditional Latin American celebration that marks a girl's transition from childhood to womanhood at age fifteen. Rooted in cultural and religious customs, the event typically includes a father-daughter dance. The dress is usually an elaborate ball gown, symbolizing the importance of the milestone.

My dress had been meant for a celebration that never happened. At fifteen, only a year after my father's passing, there was no joy in wearing it. It remained tucked away in a box, its fabric untouched, its meaning steeped in grief. I decided to transform it to stitch my past into my future. The bottom of that Quinceañera dress became the bottom of my wedding dress. It was more than just fabric. It was my way of reclaiming something unfinished, turning sorrow into beauty.

As I stood there, my mother's arm linked with mine, the weight of the moment settled over me. I had spent years longing for things to be different, wishing my father could be there. But life does not pause for grief. In that moment, I finally accepted a truth I had resisted for so long: everything in life is temporary. Nothing lasts forever. Not the joy, not the heartbreak, not even the deepest losses. Life is a series of goodbyes. It's painful, but that fragility is also what makes each moment sacred.

That understanding didn't erase the ache of my father's absence, but it changed something in me. Instead of focusing on what was missing, I focused on what was here. My mother beside me, strong, proud, and beautiful as ever. Daniel waiting at the end of the aisle. The dress that carried the weight of my past, now renewed. All I could do was stay present, embrace the imperfect beauty of this life, and remind myself that this moment, like all others, would pass. Once again, I was becoming something new, like a beautiful butterfly emerging from the cocoon.

I took a full semester off from medical school to stay home with Gabriela, our firstborn, during her first six months. When I returned, it was incredibly challenging. My mother watched her some days, and my mother-in-law, Gloria, helped on others. Despite their support, I felt like I was missing important milestones, and it left me torn and overwhelmed.

At the same time, Venezuela was grappling with political unrest. The country was growing increasingly unstable. In 1992, Hugo Chávez led an attempted coup against President Carlos Andrés Pérez. Though it failed, it marked the beginning of a turbulent new chapter in Venezuela's history.

This turbulence did not just affect the government; it reached into our daily lives, especially in education. The university went on strike, halting classes and disrupting clinical rotations. Hospitals, already strained by resource shortages, became even more chaotic as protests and political unrest intensified. Many of us in medical school felt caught in a system growing more unstable by the day. Clinicals were suspended at times, and the uncertainty about whether we would complete our training weighed heavily on all of us.

Gabriela was born in 1991. In 1994, after suffering a miscarriage, I gave birth to Tomás. I took another semester off to be with him, knowing these early moments with my children were ones I would never get back. Becoming a mother filled me with a joy I had never known. Holding my two beautiful, healthy children in my arms, I felt a profound sense of gratitude and happiness I had forgotten was possible. It wasn't only about love; it was the deep fulfillment of building my own family, something that was mine to nurture and protect. Motherhood softened me, but it also made me stronger. Every sleepless night, every milestone, every giggle and whispered "Mami" reminded me that despite the challenges, this was the life I had dreamed of. The weight of responsibility was real, but the joy far outweighed it. No career, no ambition, and no external achievement could compare to the privilege of having and raising them.

Although I was now a year behind my peers, having taken two semesters off, I was close to finishing medical school. But Venezuela's political crisis deepened. By 1995, Daniel and I knew that if Hugo Chávez gained control of the military and the country, we would not be able to provide the future we wanted for our children. In 1996, we made the difficult decision to leave Venezuela and move to the

United States, specifically to Indiana, where my sister and her husband, Carlos, were pursuing their doctoral degrees. We arrived with just $4,000 and fourteen suitcases, carrying our belongings, our hopes, and the quiet ache of what we had left behind.

Leaving Venezuela also meant leaving behind my medical degree, something I had spent years working toward. I was so close. Just one more year, one final internship, and I would have graduated. That loss cut deeply, and to this day, I still feel it. I won't pretend it didn't sting. I had pictured myself walking across that stage with my classmates, diploma in hand, as a tribute to everything I had endured and to the father I had lost. I had sacrificed sleep, poured myself into relentless rotations, and pushed through endless exams, all for this goal.

But when it came down to a choice between completing medical school or giving my children a better life, the answer was clear. It didn't make the decision easy, but it made it right. For a long time, I questioned whether I had failed myself or abandoned a dream that had defined so much of my identity.

With time, though, I've come to see it differently. Not as a loss, but as a turning point. Medical school was not the destination; it was the path that prepared me. It gave me the tools to grow, the insight to heal, find purpose, and shape me into the person I would become.

I applied to Indiana University's Radiation Therapy program and made the difficult decision to put my dream of becoming a doctor on hold so I could be more present for my children as we all adjusted to this new chapter of life. I still wanted to work in oncology, a field that had always stirred a deep sense of purpose in me, but in a way that allowed me to fulfill my most important role: being a mother. My babies and my family came first. My career came second.

Even without the MD behind my name, I knew that everything I had learned in medical school was still a part of me. That knowledge, those years of sacrifice and study, could never be taken away from me. I had already experienced the immense challenge of balancing school and motherhood in Venezuela.

This time, I wanted to choose a path that allowed me to be more present.

I graduated in 1999 with a Bachelor of Science in Radiation Therapy, finding a way to stay connected to my passion for healing while staying rooted in my home and family. Those first few years in the United States were incredibly hard. We had very little money and relied on the WIC program for basic necessities like food and medical checkups for Tomás and Gaby. The four of us lived in a small, on-campus apartment, sharing just one bedroom.

I went to school during the day and worked nights to help make ends meet. The kids struggled to adjust to a new culture and language, and we eventually had to delay Gaby's start in school by a year so she could catch up. It was a time of deep uncertainty, but also of incredible determination.

Life will always challenge us. But we rise again and again. No single decision defines us, and no season of loss can erase the beauty of what comes after. Though I never became a doctor in title, I built a meaningful life, one filled with purpose, healing, and love. I found other ways to help, to serve, to make a difference. In every step, I continued to honor my father's memory.

Looking back now, I see that life was gently guiding me, even when I didn't understand why things unfolded the way they did. Sometimes the most unexpected path is the one that brings us exactly where we're meant to be.

Figure 10: My wedding day with my mother and my beautiful dress

Chapter 4

The Beauty in What Remains

"The wound is the place where the Light enters you." ~ Rumi

Life in the United States was harder than we imagined. There were moments I questioned whether we had made the right decision. Having my sister living next door was a lifeline. Her support meant everything during those early days. I missed my mother deeply, knowing she was still in Venezuela, alone in a country that was growing increasingly dangerous. I worried about her constantly, feeling torn between the life we were trying to build and the family we had left behind.

Despite the challenges, life in Indiana was a marked improvement from what we had known. It wasn't easy, we had to adjust to a new culture, a new rhythm, and an unfamiliar way of living, but there was a sense of freedom we had never experienced before. There were no locks on the doors, just a simple turn knob. No bars on the windows. We even managed to buy a small car. Slowly, we began to see the fruits of our labor. We cherished the safety and sense of possibility that came with our new life. Our next goal was to bring my mother to the United States so she, too, could experience this freedom.

Daniel stayed with me and the children for about four months before returning to Venezuela to sell our home and manage unfinished responsibilities. We were far too young to grasp the weight of the life we were building or the complexity of the steps we had taken. We were naive and lonely, each of us trying to navigate the unfamiliar terrain of distance, parenthood, and obligation.

Then, like a violent storm crashing over a calm sea, infidelity struck our marriage.

The following years felt like trying to piece together shards of glass, fragile, sharp, and painful. We endured countless hours of counseling, each session peeling back layers of hurt that had never been spoken aloud. I buried myself in books, searching for wisdom, clinging to the hope that understanding might ease the ache. Some days, we wanted to give up. It would have been easier to walk away. But as the waves of anger and grief came and went, we discovered something buried beneath the wreckage: a belief that our marriage was still worth fighting for. We chose to stay. We chose to rebuild. We let honesty and forgiveness clear the ground for a new beginning.

Looking back, I see that sometimes life delivers storms not to destroy us but to clear the way for something stronger to grow. Healing was neither tidy nor quick. It was messy and painful, but it taught us resilience and grace. Our story didn't end in ruins. It became a story of revival. If you're fighting for something you know in your heart is worth it, don't let the noise around you convince you to quit. Let the pain shape you, let the hardship test your courage, and let love the kind that survives the fire reveal its strength. That was the love my parents had. It was the love I longed for, too.

During this time, I wasn't just heartbroken. I was furious. My anger wasn't only directed at Daniel or the situation we were in, it was directed at God. I couldn't understand why this was happening to me. Hadn't I endured enough? Hadn't I survived the loss of my father, the grief that followed, the upheaval of immigration, the sacrifices, and all the heartache that came with starting over again and again? Why did it feel like God was picking on me?

I wanted to scream. I wanted to beg for mercy. I needed answers. Why was I being tested once more? It felt unfair. Unjust. Cruel.

Up until that moment, my faith had been my anchor. It carried me through losing my father, moving to a new country, and rebuilding my life from the ground up. I leaned on it like a lifeline, trusting that God wouldn't give me more than I could handle. But this time, I wasn't sure I had the strength left. I just wanted God to pick someone else for once.

In the silence that followed my rage, I discovered something deeper than I expected. There was a quiet resolve, a willingness to face the pain without letting it shape the rest of my life. I came to understand that I could be angry at God and still cling to hope. I could wrestle with doubt and still believe that something meaningful could emerge from the wreckage. It took time, but I slowly began to see that faith isn't about never questioning—it's about finding the strength to move forward in spite of the questions.

Healing our marriage took more than time or forgiveness. It required confronting my own anger, acknowledging that I didn't have all the answers, and accepting that I might never fully understand why things unfolded the way they did. During that turbulent chapter, I turned to books. They became my sanctuary. Each one offered a new lens, a glimmer of light, or a lesson that gently nudged me toward healing. These stories and teachings became my silent companions, guiding me through heartbreak, self-discovery, and growth. Here are some of the books that helped shape my journey:

- *The Mountain Is You* by **Brianna Wiest** - Confronting self-sabotage and turning obstacles into growth.

- *Water for Elephants* by **Sara Gruen** - A story of love and survival under the big top.

- *A New Earth: Awakening to Your Life's Purpose* by **Eckhart Tolle** - Discovering a deeper sense of self beyond ego.

- *The Secret* by **Rhonda Byrne** - Manifesting dreams through the power of thought.

- *Ninety Minutes in Heaven* by **Don Piper** - A glimpse into life after death and the resilience of the human spirit.

- *Proof of Heaven* by **Dr. Eben Alexander** - A neurosurgeon's journey into the afterlife.

- *Emotional Blackmail* by **Susan Forward** - Breaking free from manipulation and guilt.

- *Tuesdays with Morrie* by **Mitch Albom** - Life lessons from a dying mentor.

- ***Believe It*** **by Jamie Kern Lima** - A journey of resilience and believing in oneself.

- ***The Biology of Belief*** **by Dr. Bruce H. Lipton** - How beliefs influence biology and health.

- ***The Science of Emotions*** **by Dr. Joe Dispenza** - Understanding the connection between thoughts and feelings.

- ***The Mastery of Love*** **by Don Miguel Ruiz** - Practical wisdom on building and sustaining love.

- ***The Four Agreements*** **by Don Miguel Ruiz** - A guide to personal freedom and breaking self-limiting beliefs.

- ***The Power of Now*** **by Eckhart Tolle** - Finding peace in the present moment.

- ***The Five People You Meet in Heaven*** **by Mitch Albom** - Reflecting on how lives intersect.

- ***The Last Lecture*** **by Randy Pausch** - An inspiring message about living with purpose.

- ***The Five Love Languages*** **by Gary Chapman** - Understanding and expressing love in relationships.

- *The Alchemist* **by Paulo Coelho** - A timeless tale about following your dreams and listening to your heart.

- *Atomic Habits* **by James Clear** - Building better habits through small, consistent changes.

- *The Year of Magical Thinking* **by Joan Didion** - An honest and profound exploration of grief and resilience.

- *The Untethered Soul* **by Michael A. Singer** - A book on mindfulness, inner peace and the nature of consciousness.

- *The Shack* **by William Paul Young** - A story of grief, faith, and forgiveness that challenged my understanding of how pain and love coexist.

Each book became a lifeline, reminding me that pain and growth often walk side by side. They taught me to summon courage, to forgive when forgiveness seemed unreachable, and to lean into the lessons life offers in its most unexpected moments. In each story and piece of wisdom, I found fragments of myself: bruised, hopeful, and slowly healing. The books didn't fix my marriage or mend my heart, but they helped me believe that both could be made whole again someday.

Amid the chaos and challenges, life offered us an unexpected blessing. In August of 2002, we welcomed one of the greatest joys of our lives: the birth of our youngest son, Alex Franco. His middle name honored my father, a decision that carried a profound and almost otherworldly sense of timing. Alex was born on my dad's birthday. It felt like a divine message, a reminder that love and legacy can outlive grief. God was showing me that even in the depths of sorrow and uncertainty, beauty and light could still emerge. Alex's arrival was a living, breathing gift, a continuation of my father's spirit through the next generation. His birth reminded me that love always finds a way to break through darkness and bring warmth to the heart.

After years of living apart, my mother was finally able to join us in the United States. At first, she settled in Houston with her sister, Tia Betty. The choice made sense. Houston's milder climate suited her, and being surrounded by family eased the transition. She found comfort in the familiarity. But as time passed, the distance from us became too difficult for her to bear. She missed her grandkids terribly. A few years later, she made the decision to move to Indiana to be closer to us. It felt like a blessing, a chance to share everyday moments and create new memories.

But Indiana, with all its promises, turned out to be a heartbreaking mistake. The brutal winters took a toll on her health almost immediately. She began suffering from frequent respiratory illnesses, and soon pneumonia returned with a vengeance. Unlike before, her body struggled to recover. Each passing year seemed to leave her weaker, more fragile. It was devastating to watch her vibrant spirit dim. Unfortunately, I had seen this decline before and recognized the signs I didn't want to acknowledge. No matter how hard we tried to protect her, the cold kept coming back, and we were powerless to stop the spiral. It was a cruel irony: wanting her near but knowing that her being here was harming her.

Eventually, her body could no longer endure the repeated strain. Despite hospital stays, medications, and every attempt to ease her suffering, her strength faded. It became clear that she could not fight much longer. We made the agonizing decision to transition her to hospice care, where she spent her final months surrounded by my sister, my Tia Betty, and me.

Becoming an orphan in my thirties was a pain I hadn't known I could survive. It was another painful, suffocating, transforming moment that crept into my life without my consent. I wasn't ready to face a world without my mother. Her absence felt like the last thread of my foundation had been pulled away, leaving me unmoored.

She was in the same hospital where I worked as a radiation therapist. During my lunch breaks, I would visit her, stealing what moments I could. I held her hand, whispered how much I loved her, and tried to soak in every second. But each day, I watched her slip further away. Her body was exhausted. She needed oxygen, then a tracheotomy, and eventually was intubated. She developed bedsores that would not heal. The decline was excruciating to witness. I struggled to reconcile the strong, graceful mother I had always known with the fragile figure lying still in the bed. I kept pushing back the thought that this was the end, even as reality settled over me, like a heavy weight.

On Mother's Day of 2007, she left us to be with Dad. That morning, after being unresponsive for several days, she opened her eyes and smiled at us. It was a beautiful, unexpected moment. We all wished her a happy Mother's Day. Her eyes held a quiet acceptance, a peace we hadn't seen in a long time. We thought she was getting better. How could that be?

The nurse gently suggested we take a short break, mentioning a special Mother's Day brunch in the hospital cafeteria. She offered to freshen Mom up and make her more comfortable while we stepped out. Reluctantly, the three of us kissed her, whispered that we loved her, and promised to be right back.

As soon as we reached the cafeteria, my phone buzzed. It was a message from the nurse urging us to return immediately. My heart dropped. We rushed back to her room. The nurse met us at the door, her face saying everything before a word was spoken. Mom was gone.

She had taken her last breath in the few minutes we were away. She had chosen that quiet moment to let go.

The nurse explained gently that this wasn't uncommon. Sometimes, loved ones wait until they are alone to take their final breath. It was as if she wanted to spare us the pain of witnessing her final breath, giving us one last gift of protection. It didn't make sense at first, and it shattered me in ways I didn't know were possible. But part of me understood. Maybe she knew we would cling too tightly. Maybe she knew we would have begged her to stay just one more day, one more hour. And she didn't want to make that goodbye even harder than it already was.

In the months that followed, I wrestled with that moment. Why didn't she want us there? How could she leave without us holding her hand? I tried to make peace with the way she chose to go. And in time, I understood: it was her final act of love. Just like when she smiled at us that morning, she had given us a gift. A moment of beauty. A memory wrapped in warmth and love.

All I could think about afterward was the day I would see my parents again. I held onto the hope that somewhere beyond this life, they were together once more, free from pain and separation. Grief clung to me like a second skin, and I was left trying to figure out how to move forward without the two people who had shaped me.

After Mom passed, I couldn't bear to stay at the hospital where she had taken her last breath. The memories were too heavy, too raw. I needed a fresh start, a place to rebuild without being surrounded by reminders of loss. That's when I joined the team at CyberKnife of Indianapolis. Looking back, it was one of the best decisions I could have made.

The years that followed were some of the happiest and most fulfilling of my career. The team felt like family. With Jody, Dr. Lord, Neal, and

Michelle, we created something truly special. We worked hard, laughed often, and supported each other through every challenge as we learned to operate a highly advanced radiosurgery system. Life felt good again. I was thriving at work, the kids were doing great, and our family felt strong and connected. I had found my footing, and for the first time in a long time, I felt truly happy.

Then, without warning, CyberKnife closed. I was laid off. The news hit me like a punch to the gut. I hadn't seen it coming, and just like that, I was adrift again, uncertain of where to go or what to do next.

One day, while driving and trying to make sense of everything, I heard a radio ad for Marian University's accelerated online BSN program. Something about it caught my attention, maybe it was the idea of starting over or the sense of purpose that nursing had held for me during the years my mother was sick. Curious and desperate for direction and craving a sense of meaning, I decided to look into it.

That decision set me on a new path, one that would challenge me, change me, and ultimately bring me full circle back to healing, but with a deeper understanding of endurance and transformation.

When I look back on those years, I can't help but ask: *What was it all for?* What is the purpose of loss? Of changes that tear away the familiar and leave you standing in the wreckage, forced to build something new? It's a question that haunted me. But somewhere along the way, I found my answer.

With every loss came a choice: to crumble or to rise.

I learned that change doesn't just strip away what we know, it makes space for what we're meant to become. It demands strength, tests our courage, and calls us to keep our hearts open, even when we're afraid of being hurt again. Life doesn't promise comfort or certainty. But it does offer us the chance to begin again. To rebuild. To discover strengths, we never knew we had.

My purpose wasn't just to endure. It was to evolve; to take pain and let it shape something meaningful. To let heartbreak deepen my empathy. To let uncertainty sharpen my resolve.

Healing, I realized, isn't just recovery. It's transformation.

It's about meeting life with an open heart, even when it's bruised. It's about trusting that the detours, the losses, and the unexpected turns are all guiding us toward a deeper version of ourselves, one that is braver, wiser, and more persevering than you ever thought possible. Sometimes life breaks you open, not to destroy you, but to expand your capacity to love, to forgive, and to grow.

Sometimes life doesn't make sense in the moment. It's only in hindsight that the broken pieces begin to form a mosaic: how moving to a new country gave me grit, how betrayal taught me what I truly valued, how losing my mother forced me to carry on with grace, and how being laid off led me to reinvent myself once again.

The meaning of life isn't found in the safety of what we already know. It lives in our ability to rise when the ground shifts beneath us. It's about keeping an open heart, even when it hurts, and seeing the opportunities disguised as challenges. Change may feel like a loss, but it also holds the potential to make us stronger, braver, and more determined to live fully.

Chapter 5

Believe You Can and You're Halfway There

"The meaning of life is to find your gift. The purpose of life is to give it away." ~ **Pablo Picasso**

One of the stories that shaped my understanding of courage and curiosity comes from my step-grandfather, Carlos Freeman. Long before I truly understood the meaning of legacy, I grew up hearing whispers about his role in something extraordinary: the discovery of Ángel Falls, the tallest waterfall in the world.

In the 1930s, my step-grandfather joined the legendary expedition with Jimmie Angel, the American pilot who crash-landed his small plane on top of Auyán Tepui, one of Venezuela's massive tabletop mountains. From that wild and dangerous landing, the world came to know the towering cascade that would become known as Salto Ángel, a waterfall so high the water turns to mist before it reaches the jungle floor. Even now, it remains a remote and sacred place, hidden deep within Canaima National Park.

Carlos Freeman passed away when I was very young, but my mother shared his stories with us. She told us that he rarely spoke about that journey, but when he did, there was a reverence in his voice. He described the dense jungle, the deafening roar of the water, and the way time seemed to pause in the presence of something so powerful.

The story of Ángel Falls is not just part of Venezuela's history. It's part of my family's history. Knowing that my own step-grandfather once stood at the top of that waterfall, long before the rest of the world knew it existed, connects me deeply to the land where I was born. I carry his legacy every time I seek out wonder, every time I stand at the edge of something vast and choose to say yes to the unknown.

Losing both of my parents has been the most profound and painful experience of my life. Their deaths taught me that grief isn't something you move on from, it's something you learn to live with. I've come to understand that loss doesn't break you. It reshapes you. It leaves behind a quieter version of yourself, one that knows the fragility of time and the value of every fleeting moment. I've learned that love and courage don't end with death; they simply take on a different form, living on through memories, through stories, and in the way we choose to carry their legacy forward.

Their passing forced me to face my fears and my strength, to stand in the space where they once were, and to find the tenacity to keep moving. It reminded me that life doesn't wait for us to be ready, and healing doesn't come with a roadmap. Healing is a choice to keep loving, to keep living, and to believe in yourself and the purpose of your life, even in the absence of those you've lost.

Loss demands that we begin again and again, in ways we never imagined we'd have to. It is a kind of metamorphosis an evolution of the soul. You are cracked open, made vulnerable, and asked to transform in a tight, dark space whether you feel ready or not. I had to shed a version of myself that no longer fit. I had to allow the pain to shape me into someone new, someone braver and more resilient even when I could no longer recognize my reflection. In that unraveling, I became curious about my family's past. I wanted to understand what those who came before me had endured.

There's an unexpected guilt that arises when suffering finally begins to loosen its grip. After Mom passed, I found myself relieved that the nightmare was over, that the endless days and nights of worry and watching her struggle to breathe had come to an end. But then came the guilt. How could I feel relief when the cost of that peace was losing her?

It took time to understand that healing doesn't mean it never happened. It doesn't erase the pain or the memories. Healing means I found a way to keep going, to breathe without feeling like I was drowning. Sometimes, it meant allowing myself to feel peace without questioning whether I deserved it or where it came from.

Starting a new career in my forties gave me a chance to reinvent myself once again, and I was good at it. Losing my dad at such a young age left an indelible mark. It planted a fear deep inside me, a fear that something could happen to my family without warning. That fear is why I never wanted to be a stay-at-home mom. When CyberKnife closed and I was faced with that possibility, I needed to know I could stand on my own two feet. I needed to know I could provide and survive if life ever pulled the rug out from under me again.

I didn't want to be home with the kids not because I didn't love them, but because I knew how quickly everything could change. What would I do if something happened to my husband?

Loss reshapes how you see the world. It changes how you protect yourself and how you choose to move forward. It took years for me to realize that starting over doesn't mean starting from scratch.

I applied to Marian University's accelerated BSN program with a mix of excitement and nerves. In my forties, I was embarking on what would become my third career. Although all my professional paths had centered around health, healing, and service, this was something entirely new. It felt like starting over, and with that came the familiar fear of the unknown. But I also felt ready for the challenge. I was determined to prove to myself that I could take on nursing and thrive.

Despite the nerves, I threw myself into the program with everything I had. Sixteen intense months later, I graduated magna cum laude, a moment that filled me with pride and affirmed that I could still accomplish big things, no matter my age or how often life asked me to begin again.

I was honored to give the class pinning speech, sharing words of hope with my fellow graduates.

And to top it all off, I received the Peer Mentor Award, a recognition that meant so much because it came from the very people who had walked beside me through that journey.

This wasn't just about earning another degree. It was about reclaiming my confidence. It was about proving that no matter how many times I had to begin again, I would always find the strength to move forward with my head held high.

My first nursing job was in the Radiation Therapy department at Parkview Hospital in Fort Wayne. It felt like life had come full circle. I was working alongside Neal from CyberKnife again, sharing space with someone who had been part of some of the most rewarding years of my professional journey. I loved being back in that environment, immersed in patient care, surrounded by a team that felt like family.

The only challenge was the commute. I was driving two hours each way, five days a week. During those long drives, I often reflected on how far I had come and where this new path might lead. After a few months, a new opportunity opened up at Community Cancer Center South. They needed a manager to build a new department from the ground up. The idea was both thrilling and intimidating. Still, I knew I was ready to shape something meaningful, to create a space where patients would receive not just treatment, but dignity and compassionate care.

I poured myself into the work, guided by a vision of excellence and service. One of my proudest accomplishments was helping the department earn the prestigious MD Anderson certification. It was a powerful affirmation that we were providing cancer care at the highest standard.

I'll never forget visiting MD Anderson as part of that process. Walking those halls stirred something deep in me. It was there that my father had undergone surgery so many years before. Being back in that place, now as a nurse and leader, was both surreal and sacred. I could feel my father's presence. I silently promised to carry his spirit with me in every patient interaction, in every decision I made from that day forward.

Despite the pride I felt in my role as a manager, I began to miss the hands-on work. The heart of why I had become a radiation therapist, and later, a nurse was calling me back. I missed the closeness with patients, the quiet moments of comfort, and the sense of purpose that came from direct care.

Eventually, I made the difficult decision to leave that leadership role and accept a position in the Neonatal Intensive Care Unit at Riley Hospital. It was a shift I hadn't expected, but one that felt aligned with what my heart needed.

The NICU was unlike anything I had experienced. I was now caring for the tiniest, most fragile humans surrounded by beeping monitors, sterile incubators, and the softest cries. It was physically draining and emotionally intense, but it was also deeply purposeful. There were long nights and stressful shifts, but there was also a fierce dedication to seeing those little fighters pull through.

Through it all, I learned that strength doesn't always come from heroic acts.

The NICU taught me that vulnerability and strength can coexist, and that sometimes the smallest souls teach us the most profound lessons about courage and hope.

During this time, I found myself longing for peace, the kind of quiet that this high-adrenaline job simply didn't offer. The NICU demanded constant alertness, and the rush of baby codes kept my body and mind in perpetual fight-or-flight mode. My soul ached for stillness, a way to balance the chaos and find some calm. That's when I discovered yoga.

At first, it was just a way to stretch out the tension after a long shift. But soon, I realized it was more than just movement, it was medicine. Each class became a sacred space where I could engage my parasympathetic system and feel my heart rate slow, my breathing deepen. After being surrounded by beeping monitors and fragile lives for hours on end, stepping onto the mat was like stepping into a sanctuary of my own making. I practiced for months, each session grounding me, helping me find balance, and offering a release I didn't know I needed. I became so fascinated by how I felt after each class, the way peace seemed to settle into my bones and soften the edges of my stress, that I decided to go all in. I wanted to understand it, live it, and eventually share it. That's when I made the decision to obtain my 200-hour yoga teacher certification.

Recalling this time of my life, it seems almost laughable, could I possibly add anything else to my plate? Between my nursing career, being a mom, and navigating life's endless demands, I had already proven to myself time and again that I could do hard things. This addition was something that brought me peace. I was surrendering and trusting that this would heal me. Yoga wasn't just a practice, it became a lifeline, a way to connect to myself in a world that constantly demanded more. And I knew that if I could share that feeling with others, it might just make the world a little lighter for someone else too.

Around this time, I also discovered hot yoga, and let me tell you there is nothing quite like it. The moment you walk in, the heat wraps around you like a blanket, intense, yes, but comforting in its own way. The outside world starts to melt, and you shift into yourself. This practice is about staying present when things get uncomfortable. Wow! Could I relate to this!

In the heat, you can't hide from your breath. You meet yourself fully, layer by layer. For me, hot yoga is more than a workout, it's a mental and emotional release. I've cried on my mat, I've laughed quietly at the resistance my body offers, and I've come out the other side lighter, stronger, more in tune with what I truly need. This practice helps me refill my cup. It's where I process. It's where I heal. The Hot Room in Indianapolis is where this magic happens.

Working in the NICU made me realize just how much I loved working with kids, but as much as I cherished those moments, I also knew that realistically, I couldn't sustain that level of stress forever. I wanted more time with my own kids and the flexibility to enjoy life outside of work. That's when I made the decision to continue my pediatric nursing career as a school nurse. It felt like the perfect solution, still working with children but without the relentless, high-pressure of the NICU. Plus, it offered the incredible gift of time off in the summer and holidays to be with my family. It was the kind of balance I needed, and it felt like I was finally moving toward a lifestyle that allowed me to be present for my own kids.

During this time, I also obtained a Yoga for Cancer (y4c) certification, taught by Tari Prinster in New York. Teaching yoga to people navigating cancer is the most humbling, heart-expanding class I teach.

I've been teaching oncology yoga since 2016, and every class reminds me that strength doesn't always look like holding a pose, it often looks like showing up, taking a deep breath, and choosing gentleness over force. Many of my students are in active treatment or recovery. Some arrive in wigs, others are caregivers or survivors finding their way back to their bodies. We don't push. We listen to the body, to the breath, to the moment. The focus is always on empowerment through mindful movement, breathwork, and rest. We modify everything. We meet each person exactly where they are physically, emotionally, and energetically. It's not about yoga poses. It's about presence.

I don't just teach them, they teach me. Every. Single. Time. This work has shaped me and it's one of the great honors of my life to hold that space.

Working as an elementary school nurse came with its own challenges. I had a busy clinic that averaged about 70 kids a day, each one bringing their own unique challenges and stories. I was responsible for everything from administering daily medications to managing feeding tubes, handling injuries, treating fevers, and dealing with illnesses. We also had students with chronic conditions like diabetes and seizure disorders, and it was my job to make sure they were safe, healthy, and supported throughout the school day. I became an expert in quick triage and gentle reassurance. There were the kids who came to the clinic not because they were sick but because they needed a little extra *TLC*, a few minutes to sit quietly, a reassuring word, or just someone to listen to their worries. Some would come in for a stomach ache that magically disappeared after a little bit of attention. I knew that sometimes they just needed to feel safe and cared for, and I was happy to be that comforting presence. It didn't take long to realize that being a school nurse wasn't just about medical care, it was about being a steady, dependable source of comfort in their world. The clinic became a refuge for some, a place where they could let down their guard and feel seen. And as much as I gave to them, they gave back to me tenfold.

One student that comes to mind, who had a profound impact on my life, was Logan. He was a mischievous, spirited 5th grade kid with a smile that could light up a room and a stubborn streak that matched his fiery energy. Logan was diabetic, and managing his blood sugars was a daily battle. Sometimes his numbers would skyrocket for no apparent reason, leaving me frustrated and worried. I suspected he might be sneaking snacks on the bus or during recess, but he would never admit it. Instead, his teacher would bring him storming into the clinic, angry and defiant, while I calmly called his care team to get instructions on how to address his dangerously high blood sugar levels.

We had to check the ketones in his urine regularly, and I couldn't help but feel the weight of responsibility pressing down on me. I knew what uncontrolled diabetes could do to his kidneys over time, and the thought haunted me. I would sit with him, trying to explain to him the dangers of what was happening and trying to understand why he wouldn't take better care of himself. Sometimes he would listen, and sometimes he would just glare at me, resentful and angry. I understood that he was just a kid, trying to navigate the unfairness of having to manage something so big at such a young age.

One day, while checking his ketones and mentally running through the worst-case scenarios, a thought hit me like a bolt of lightning, what if Logan ever needed a kidney transplant? I would give him one of mine without hesitation. I didn't even question it, it was just a visceral, undeniable truth that settled in my heart. He didn't need one, of course Logan was still healthy despite his struggles but that thought planted a seed in me that had been quietly growing for years. What if I could help someone else in need? Another child whose kidneys were failing, who was out of options?

It wasn't long after that moment that I began to seriously consider becoming a living kidney donor. It wasn't about Logan specifically, but about the realization that I could be the answer to someone's prayer. Maybe my story, my path, was meant to lead me here, to give a part of myself to save someone else's life. I know that Logan didn't just impact my life because of his tenacity or his spirit, he changed me because he sparked the idea that would alter the course of my own story. That moment in the clinic became the catalyst for something far greater, a decision that would shape my life and the lives of others in ways I couldn't have imagined.

Sometimes, in the chaos and noise of life, the only way forward is to sit in the silence and let the heart speak. The heart knows the way, even when the path ahead is uncertain and filled with fear. In those moments, I would reflect on the choices I had made, the lives I had touched, and the lessons that had shaped me. One quote always echoed in my heart, a reminder of the power of human connection: *"To the world, you may be one person, but to one person, you may be the world."* — Dr. Seuss.

I never set out to change the world, but I knew that changing even one life mattered. Whether it was caring for a fragile newborn in the NICU, comforting a child in the school clinic, or considering the gift of life through kidney donation, I knew that to someone, I could make ALL the difference.

When the life I envisioned kept falling apart, I knew that every heartbreak, every unexpected turn, every challenge was guiding me to where I was meant to be. It was about understanding that growth happens through discomfort and that there is power in choosing to believe in something better. It took courage to let go of what I thought life should be and embrace the unknown. There were moments when doubt crept in, when I questioned whether to keep starting over. Believing I could make it through was half the battle, and once I let that belief sink in, the rest was just taking one step at a time.

Life will always be unpredictable and messy, but choosing to believe you can overcome it, is preparing you for something greater. If you believe you can, you're already halfway there. The thought of living kidney donation felt like roots spreading deep into the ground, anchoring me in a way that felt unshakable. Roots give us stability; they hold us steady when life tries to uproot us. And just as roots ground a tree, my desire to make a difference became an anchor that I couldn't ignore. I couldn't quite explain it at the time, but I knew in my heart that I would change someone's life forever.

Living kidney donation wasn't just a fleeting thought or a reckless impulse, it was a deep, profound calling that wouldn't let go of me. I understood the gravity of what it meant, the risks involved, and the lifelong impact it could have. I wasn't naïve to reality, but I also knew that I needed to learn more and to do my research fully. The seed had been planted long ago, and now it was taking root, becoming a part of me that I couldn't ignore, no matter how daunting it seemed. I felt drawn to explore this possibility, not out of obligation but from a place of purpose, and even though I wasn't ready to take the leap just yet, I knew in my soul that one day I would. I just needed to prepare and trust that when the time came, I would be ready to follow my heart.

Figure 11: Angel Falls

Chapter 6

Creating Ripples of Hope

"We make a living by what we get, but we make a life by what we give." ~

Winston Churchill

To Remember Me - I Will Live Forever: by Robert Noel Test (1926-1994). "The day will come when my body will lie upon a white sheet neatly tucked under four corners of a mattress located in a hospital; busily occupied with the living and the dying. At a certain moment a doctor will determine that my brain has ceased to function and that, for all intents and purposes, my life has stopped.

When that happens, do not attempt to instill artificial life into my body by the use of a machine.

And don't call this my deathbed. Let it be called the bed of life, and let my body be taken from it to help others lead fuller lives.

Give my sight to the man who has never seen a sunrise, a baby's face or love in the eyes of a woman.

Give my heart to a person whose own heart has caused nothing but endless days of pain.

Give my blood to the teenager who was pulled from the wreckage of his car, so that he might live to see his grandchildren play.

Give my kidneys to the one who depends on a machine to exist from week to week.

Take my bones, every muscle, every fiber and nerve in my body and find a way to make a crippled child walk. Explore every corner of my brain.

Take my cells, if necessary, and let them grow so that, someday a speechless boy will shout at the crack of a bat and a deaf girl will hear the sound of rain against her window.

Burn what is left of me and scatter the ashes to the winds to help the flowers grow.

If you must bury something, let it be my faults, my weakness and all prejudice against my fellow man.

Give my sins to the devil. Give my soul to God. If, by chance, you wish to remember me, do it with a kind deed or word to someone who needs you. If you do all I have asked, I will live forever."

Robert N. Test was one of the pioneers in promoting organ and tissue donations.

I've always been the type to see the glass as half full rather than half empty. Living with purpose and following my heart, trusting that I am exactly where I'm meant to be, has given my life so much meaning. So, I encourage anyone reading this, don't be afraid of change. Instead, lean into it, knowing that growth lies on the other side of fear.

In 2016, I began my journey of discovering the world of living kidney donation. I wasn't sure if I would be healthy enough to donate, I was 48 years old. I knew that giving a kidney wasn't something to take lightly and my own health had to come first. There was a part of me that feared the tests might reveal something unexpected, something that would disqualify me from donating and bring my journey to an abrupt halt.

Before I ever began the official process of kidney donation, I spent about six months deeply researching it. I read medical journals, donor stories, watched videos, and even connected with people who had gone through it. I needed to be sure, not just about the impact on the recipient, but on my own long-term health. The idea had been planted years earlier, but it wasn't until I felt ready that I took the first step.

The testing process began with a basic blood draw to determine compatibility. Even though I was pursuing a non-directed donation, meaning I didn't know who would receive my kidney, they still needed to assess my blood type and tissue typing to begin the matching process.

The first blood draw after that turned into 14 tubes of blood. They checked everything from kidney function to infectious diseases, cholesterol levels, liver enzymes, blood sugar, you name it.

Next came imaging and cardiac testing:

- Chest X-ray, to check my lungs and make sure there were no hidden concerns.

- EKG, to rule out any heart issues that could make surgery risky.

- Pap smear and mammogram, since I was over 40, to ensure there were no undetected cancers or abnormalities.

Once I cleared the first wave of labs and tests, I met with an entire transplant team. Every specialist had a specific role to play in advocating for my safety and ensuring I was truly ready for this decision:

- A psychologist, who asked deep and thoughtful questions. Why did I want to do this? How did my family feel? Did I understand the donation process? Did I have support at home? It wasn't a quiz, it was more like an emotional checkpoint, and I appreciated the care they took.

- A dietitian, who reviewed my eating habits and ensured I could maintain kidney health with just one kidney post-surgery.

- A living donor advocate, one of the most important people in the process. Their sole job is to look out for the donor's best interest. They made it clear that I could stop the process at any point, even the day before surgery, and it would be respected.

- A nephrologist, who looked at the function of both kidneys and my general health history. They made sure I wasn't prediabetic, hypertensive, or at risk for chronic disease down the road.

- The living donor coordinator, the RN who managed the process from beginning to end, reviewed my results, tests and coordinated the next steps.

- The transplant surgeon, who's responsible for removing the kidney from the donor.

One of the more fascinating tests was the renal scan, which evaluates how much each kidney contributes to total kidney function. The results showed one kidney doing slightly more work than the other, so they decided to leave me with the stronger one. That alone reassured me—they weren't just taking any kidney. They were looking out for my future, too.

After all the evaluations, my case was presented to a multidisciplinary transplant committee. Surgeons, nephrologists, nurses, social workers, and psychologists all had to approve. It wasn't until every single person said yes that I was officially cleared to donate.

I passed every test, proving not only to the medical team but to myself that I was ready and capable of taking this step. With each hurdle cleared, my confidence grew. I was healthy. I was strong. I was ready to give this gift.

It felt surreal, almost as if the universe had been waiting for me to catch up to the calling that had been whispering for years. There was relief and gratitude in knowing that my body was capable of giving life—but also a deep sense of responsibility. I couldn't help but feel that this had been part of my path all along, a chance to turn the pain of losing my father into hope for someone else. I heard a quiet message within: *You couldn't save him, but you can save someone else's father, brother, son.*

It was about choosing to believe that we are here not just to endure, but to give. To create ripples of hope that extend far beyond ourselves, touching lives in ways we may never fully understand. The idea of giving someone a second chance at life lit something within me. It awakened my soul.

I will never forget the day I finally found the courage to tell my family: "I'm donating my kidney." The words came out with more conviction than I expected. I hadn't rehearsed them, but there they were, spoken and irreversible. It felt both terrifying and beautiful.

I watched their faces closely, searching for signs of support, worry, or understanding. I needed their love, not permission.

"What?" my husband said, his voice filled with disbelief.

Still, I felt a surge of purpose rise within me.

"I've been thinking about this for a long time. I've done a lot of research, and I've gone through every test. I've been approved to donate to a complete stranger," I said, my voice laced with excitement and certainty.

I've always been the one to embrace challenges, just like my great-grandmother or my step-grandfather. I've taken leaps where others might hesitate. This decision wasn't impulsive. I had studied every step, considered every complication, reviewed every statistic. I wasn't walking into this lightly. I was walking in with open eyes and an open heart.

At first, my family was hesitant. Their concerns were natural. But they also knew me. They knew that once I made up my mind, there was no turning back. I wasn't seeking approval. I only hoped for their support.

I was choosing the life I wanted, a life of purpose. A life that transformed pain into something meaningful. I had carried the grief of losing my father for so long, haunted by the helplessness of not being able to save him. Now I had the chance to give that gift of life to someone else's father, someone's child, someone's loved one. How could I ignore a calling like that?

I remember arriving at the hospital at 11:45 a.m. on a Wednesday, 15 minutes ahead of my appointment. I was there to meet Dr. John A. Powelson, Professor of Surgery. I had researched him meticulously, studying his degrees, honors, awards, and medical achievements. I was prepared, almost like a detective following the threads of a complex mystery.

As I waited, I sent a gentle text to my husband: "Please try not to be late."

It was a small reminder, something I often said with love. He tended to run behind schedule, a habit he had carried from his days growing up in Venezuela. His occasional lateness sometimes sparks a hint of unease in me.

"I'm on my way," he texted back. Unsure if I fully believed him, his effort brought a smile to my face.

He knew today was significant for me, and that was what truly mattered.

On the fourth floor of IU Health University Hospital in Indianapolis, a large silver sign reading "Organ Transplant" greets me as the elevator doors open. Behind it lies an open, oval waiting room. Standard and recliner chairs, covered in faux leather with a few creases and scratches, mingle with scattered tables holding random magazines and brochures. A TV on the wall airs local news, while a digital screen shares staff information, offering a touch of amusement. The decor, reminiscent of the 1980s, reflects the typical style of a teaching hospital—nothing overly fancy. Bright, evenly distributed light washes over sterile, uninviting white walls. Medical codes and overhead pages fill the air. Most occupants are middle-aged patients waiting patiently, some with a grayish tint to their skin, others as bright and cheery as myself. I wonder about their stories, how long they've been unwell or why they're here, and if they wonder the same about me.

"Cristina Fontana!" calls out a middle-aged, tall, slender, and somewhat reserved man, holding a medical chart.

"That's me!" I reply, raising my hand like a student answering a teacher's call as I make my way to him.

"John Powelson, nice to meet you," he says with a firm voice, offering a handshake.

"Very nice to meet you," I reply with a shy smile.

Daniel arrives fifteen minutes late, but with Dr. Powelson delayed by a lengthy surgery, I've forgotten about his tardiness. After introducing himself, we follow Dr. Powelson to his office, hand in hand as always, my cold, sweaty hands enveloped in his firm, comforting grip.

His office is small, well-lit, and impeccably organized. A simple wooden desk holds stacks of papers and charts. The walls display diplomas, certificates, and framed achievements. A large pearl-gray yoga core ball serves as his desk chair, piquing my curiosity. As soon as the door closes, he greets me with a warm smile. Is this the same doctor who intimidated me moments ago?

In a composed and gentle manner, he explains the planned surgery, discussing potential risks and expected outcomes. He patiently addresses our questions and concerns, especially Daniel's fear of losing me during surgery or my liver being harmed since I'm donating my right kidney.

"I have never lost a patient," he reassures him. His ability to explain complex medical information with compassion and clarity instills confidence and trust in both of us.

We're asked to watch a video about living with a single kidney, stressing the importance of caring for the remaining kidney post-donation. Dr. Powelson examines my abdomen closely and reviews my lab results. I can feel his dedication to his patients, and that means the world to me.

"You're a nurse?" he asks with a curious tone. "Do you know what happens to your remaining kidney after surgery?" he continues.

I nod, already familiar with the answer, and he seems a little surprised.

He spends over an hour with us. We never feel rushed. The meeting becomes a turning point—offering the reassurance my husband needs to fully support a decision I've already made in my heart.

Just before we leave, my heart races with a blend of nerves and hope. Gathering my courage, I ask Dr. Powelson something personal. The intimidating air he carried at the start of the appointment has softened. In its place is warmth, trust, and a shared understanding.

"Would it be possible to play a song for me while I'm being put to sleep?" I ask, unsure if the request is appropriate.

He pauses, his hands still on the chart, and looks up with genuine interest.

"Go on," he says.

"I don't remember much about my father, but I do remember him singing *'O Sole Mio'* by Luciano Pavarotti. I'd like to hear it before the surgery starts."

A gentle smile spreads across his face, and he nods with understanding.

"You'll need to bring your phone and give it to the nurse," he says, his voice kind.

In that moment, I know he understands not just the request, but the meaning behind it. I'm not simply a patient. I'm a daughter honoring her father's memory. A woman on a mission that defies logic and embraces love.

His response tells me everything: that he sees the humanity in this moment, the weight of the story behind my decision. For the first time, I feel completely seen.

I leave that meeting stronger than ever.

On January 25, 2018, I donated my right kidney to a complete stranger.

To my surprise, the recovery was gentler than expected. I went home the very next day. The first few days were hard, but once I was back in my own bed, surrounded by the quiet support of my family, healing began to unfold. Slowly, steadily, I regained my strength.

Within twelve weeks, I was back to my normal routine, grateful for the resilience of my body and the unwavering encouragement of those who walked beside me. It felt as though my body understood the purpose of this gift and responded with grace.

Then, something unexpected happened. A new door opened, almost too perfect to be coincidence.

I was offered a position as a Living Donor Coordinator.

My journey with kidney donation had just begun, and already I found myself immersed in a world where lives were changed every day by selfless acts, acts like mine. I was honored to join the same team that had supported me through my own donation.

My lifelong love of learning kicked in again, urging me forward. I wanted to understand more, to advocate harder, to inspire deeply.

I became more than a non-directed donor.

I became a voice of hope, of experience, of possibility.

Unlike others, I knew firsthand what it felt like to lie on that table. I could speak not just as a nurse, but as someone who had lived it.

It didn't take long for me to realize that my love for teaching and inspiring others was just as strong as my passion for health and healing. The more I shared what I had learned, the more fulfillment I found in helping others understand the transformative power of giving. Writing became an outlet, a way to process my fears and share the story that was unfolding before me.

I started to see my father in every recipient I met. In the way their eyes lit up with gratitude. In the way their families clung to hope, believing this gift might give them more time. I couldn't save my father, but through this journey, I was helping other people's fathers. That realization opened my eyes to the deeper purpose behind my decision.

I hadn't just given a kidney. I had given hope to hundreds of other families through my work as a nurse. And in that giving, I was healing too, healing the part of me that had always felt powerless in the face of loss.

Deciding to share my story publicly wasn't easy. Vulnerability had never come naturally to me. But I knew that if even one person felt inspired to consider donation or to support someone through the process, it would be worth it. I shared my experience with some of my patients, but not all. Eventually, I found Kidney Donor Athletes (KDA) and connected with people who understood. They knew the drive to give, the passion for pushing limits even after giving a part of themselves. It was like finding a second family, one that spoke the same language of courage and commitment in a way my own family couldn't fully grasp.

My kidney went to a young Hispanic boy named Francisco. It's strange how easily you can love a complete stranger. From the moment I stepped into his room, I knew he was someone special. It was effortless to want nothing more than to see him thrive. He was the same age as my children, and it felt as though I had given life to another son. He helped me understand that love doesn't always come from familiarity. Sometimes, it comes from recognizing the humanity in someone else's struggle and choosing to walk beside them.

I believed I could make a difference. The rest was simply letting love and purpose guide me, one step at a time.

In 2020, while working as a transplant nurse, the COVID-19 pandemic shook the world. It was a time of unprecedented change and uncertainty. Life suddenly felt fragile, and everything we knew shifted overnight. For me, the pandemic reinforced the urgency of health and adaptability. It reminded me again how quickly life can change and how essential it is to be willing to change with it.

We began to appreciate our health and each other in ways we hadn't before. It was a time that demanded we dig deep, not just for ourselves but for one another.

It was an incredibly difficult time to be a nurse. I witnessed overwhelming loss as the virus swept through our hospitals. Transplant surgeries were paused. Immunosuppressed patients succumbed to the virus. Those who survived often lost their grafts because we had to adjust their medications to keep them alive. The weight of so much loss was almost unbearable. I watched people die alone, without the comfort of their families, due to strict visitation rules.

My own family was not spared. In Italy, we lost Filippo and Stefania. At home, we lost Zach, my middle son's best friend. And Francisco, the young boy who had received my kidney, was among those who lost his transplant during the pandemic.

After not traveling to Italy for two years, I decided in 2022 that it was time to take a step back. I needed to focus on my family, our home in Italy, and myself. I knew I had to temporarily step away from the transplant world and the hospital system. Deep down, I trusted that something new would emerge when the time was right, something that would allow me to keep living out my purpose.

Chapter 7

Rising Above the Peaks

"Alone we can do so little; together we can do so much." ~ **Helen Keller**

Exploring the world has always been one of my greatest joys. There is something transformative about stepping into new cultures, tasting unfamiliar foods, and walking roads that have existed for centuries. One of my lifelong dreams has been to visit every continent and, with each journey, to feel more connected to the world and to myself.

My climb toward something greater began in Africa. Becoming a member of Kidney Donor Athletes (KDA) opened doors I never imagined. One of the most incredible opportunities was the chance to climb Mount Kilimanjaro, the tallest freestanding mountain in the world. As soon as I heard about the climb, I knew I had to be part of it. It wasn't just about reaching the summit, it was about proving to myself and to others that donating a kidney didn't mean giving up on adventure or strength. It was about raising awareness, challenging stereotypes, and showing that donors are capable of extraordinary things.

When I announced my decision to climb, something unexpected and beautiful happened. My family wanted to join me. Instead of participating with the KDA team, I found myself surrounded by my loved ones, planning an unforgettable family adventure. We trained together for an entire year, shared stories, and turned the climb into our collective mission.

The trek up Mount Kilimanjaro was unlike anything I had ever experienced. The journey began deep in the rainforest, lush, green, alive. We started at the Lemosho Gate, full of nervous energy, unsure of what lay ahead but feeling the emotion of the mountain. The path was muddy and tangled with roots. I remember thinking, "My body gets to do this." I listened to my breath, matched it to each step, and let the forest wrap around me. That night, we slept under the stars, lulled by the sounds of monkeys in the jungle.

The terrain shifted quickly as we left the rainforest and entered the heath zone. Everything felt more exposed. I could see the clouds stretch for miles. We climbed slowly "Pole Pole," as they say in Swahili. I remember feeling stronger than I expected. My body adjusted quickly, but I did not take it for granted. I drank water constantly, listened closely to the guides, and stayed attuned to every signal my body sent me. We reached Shira 1 Camp with tired legs and full hearts.

The next day brought a gradual climb across the Shira Plateau. Wide open spaces, surreal beauty. The air was thinner, but the views kept me moving. I thought of my father that day, and my kidney recipient. Every step felt like it was for them. That afternoon, we did an acclimatization hike, just enough to get the heart pumping, then descended slightly to sleep at a lower altitude. That's how we outsmart the mountain.

Day 4 was tough. The altitude hit harder than expected. We climbed to Lava Tower, over 15,000 feet, and the nausea crept in. A headache and fatigue showed up, but so did my mindset training. I reminded myself it was temporary. I reminded myself I was strong.

The descent into Barranco Camp was breathtaking. We arrived exhausted but proud. This was the day I started to believe I could truly summit.

Then came the dreaded Barranco Wall. It looked intimidating, like something out of a movie. I was afraid, and it ended up being my least favorite part of the climb. It wasn't just about physical strength. It was about strategy, coordination, trust in the guides, and trust in my footing. Every push-up, moves and side-step felt empowering. When I reached the top, the view took my breath away. After that, we continued on to Karanga Camp, where the wind howled through the night. I bundled up, layering for warmth, preparing for what was next.

The climb from Karanga to Barafu Base Camp was short but steep. We were above the clouds now, fully in summit territory. Barafu Camp sits at 15,300 feet, rocky and exposed. We arrived mid-day, ate an early dinner, and tried to rest. But no one really sleeps. I lay in the tent, my heart pounding, the cold settling into my bones, knowing we would wake around ten or eleven that night for the final push. I whispered a silent prayer to my dad, to my body, to the mountain. I was ready.

Each day brought new challenges: steep inclines, unpredictable weather, and the constant battle between determination and exhaustion.

Nothing could have prepared me for summit night. We left camp around 10:30 p.m., bundled tightly against the cold, our headlamps cutting narrow paths through the darkness. Step by step, I pushed forward against the thin air and aching muscles. Every breath felt like it was pulled through a straw. The hours stretched on. A three-mile trek with over 7,000 feet of elevation gain took more than eight hours.

I had to dig deeper than I ever had. It was the hardest thing I've ever done. The altitude was relentless, but I kept moving. Slow. Steady. Focused.

When I saw the sign at Stella Point, I cried.

At Uhuru Peak, the roof of Africa, a wave of emotion washed over me. Gratitude. Grief. Power. I had made it, with one kidney, with purpose, and with love.

Reaching the summit at sunrise, after what felt like an eternity, was pure magic. Standing at 19,341 feet, looking out over the world, I knew every step had been worth it. We took a few pictures, knowing the descent still lay ahead. Reaching the summit wasn't the end. It was only the halfway point.

The descent was brutal. Loose rocks, sore knees, and hours upon hours of trekking downhill, but nothing could take away what we had just done. The final descent. The forest came back into view, and so did the bird songs, the green, the life. We laughed more that day than we had the entire week. We signed out at the gate, greeted by the other members of our team who did not reach the summit, as well as my son Tomas and his girlfriend, Bri. We received our summit certificates, sang, danced, and took it all in. The quiet pride. The aching feet. The forever changed hearts.

After the climb, we treated ourselves to an unforgettable safari, immersing ourselves in the beauty of Africa's wildlife. Seeing elephants, lions, and giraffes roaming freely across the plains was surreal, as if nature itself was congratulating us on our accomplishment.

The safari was a fitting way to wind down after such an intense physical and emotional challenge. Sitting around the campfire under the vast, star-filled sky, I reflected on how life had led me to this moment, from a painful past to this incredible triumph. I couldn't help but feel grateful not just for the experience but for the realization that giving a part of myself hadn't limited me; it had made me stronger and more open to every adventure life has to offer.

One thing I've learned through life is that we truly rise by lifting others. Whether it's through volunteering, lending a hand, or simply showing up for someone in need, the return is always greater than the gift. Helping others fills our spirit in ways material things never could. It reminds us that we're all connected, that there's power in compassion and purpose in community. Giving isn't just about changing someone else's life; it's about transforming our own in the process.

That's why living kidney donation has become such a meaningful part of my story. The need is immense and growing. As of early 2025, nearly 90,000 people in the United States are waiting for a life-saving kidney transplant. Tragically, about 13 people die each day while still on the waiting list. The average wait time can stretch from three to five years, or even longer for certain blood types. Yet, there's hope. In 2024 alone, over 27,000 kidney transplants were performed, with more than 7,000 of those coming from living donors—people just like you and me who said yes to something bigger than themselves. On average, 132 organ transplants are performed each day, thanks to both deceased and living donors. (Source: Organ Procurement and Transplantation Network (OPTN), U.S. Department of Health and Human Services, 2025.)

Still, the gap remains wide, and the call for more living donors is louder than ever.

These numbers aren't just statistics. They represent real people. Parents. Siblings. Children. Friends. When we choose to help, to share our story, or to consider donating ourselves, we become part of the ripple effect that brings healing and hope to families across the country.

In 2023, I was given the opportunity to participate in another kidney donor advocacy trek, this time hiking to Everest Base Camp with two other living kidney donors. It all began with a marathon 14-hour flight aboard Qatar Airlines, which carried us from Chicago to Doha. Awaiting us there was a four-hour layover, during which anticipation intertwined with fatigue. As a child, I had always dreamed of summiting Mount Everest. While I knew this would never happen due to the dangers it carries, I knew this particular trek had a deep sense of purpose.

While both Doha and Kathmandu are situated in Asia, Doha has the most massive and cutting-edge airport I've ever witnessed. Each terminal is filled with luxurious amenities, where Lamborghinis are raffled off and high-end stores like Gucci, Prada, Chanel, and Armani line the terminal. Despite its grandeur, one aspect stands out—limited seating options. Surprisingly, for an airport of such magnitude, finding a place to sit is a challenge. The atmosphere is permeated with an air of affluence, and the passengers appear notably well-off.

Upon our arrival in Kathmandu, the striking contrast between Doha and Tribhuvan International Airport becomes immediately apparent. Kathmandu's airport is nestled among the picturesque Himalayan landscape, featuring very basic amenities and just a few immigration counters. The airport is filled with crowds, feeling congested and busy. We find ourselves surrounded by a sea of people, many of whom carry backpacks, unmistakably prepared for the enchanting adventure of conquering the majestic Himalayan mountains.

Navigating through immigration, presenting our proof of COVID vaccination cards, and paying for our visas proves to be a bit of a hustle. The baggage claim area is notably small with many bags left unattended. As soon as we step outside, we are greeted by what seems like millions of people holding signs with names. I can't help but wonder how we will ever locate our Embark Exploration guide.

But it was in Kathmandu where my heart landed.

"I wonder how many of these people are going to Summit Everest," I whisper to Daniel as we observe the travelers.

Daniel glances around, his eyes wide with curiosity. "You're right," he replies, "it seems like everyone here is geared up for some mountain adventure."

As we stepped out into the fresh sunny morning of March 31, 2023, our guide, *Pemba*, advised us to wear face masks due to the city's pollution. He mentions that Kathmandu is the most densely populated city in the world. The car that awaits us for the ride to the hotel is a simple white caravan, with modest air conditioning that doesn't seem to work at all. It doesn't take long for us to notice the British influence in the city, as people drive on the left side of the road, a reminder of its colonial history. Our striking first impression is the view of the Himalayan mountains.

Navigating the narrow streets of Kathmandu was like stepping into a living painting. Electricity wires dangled overhead in wild tangles. This sight prompts me to quickly snap my very first picture!

"Look, Daniel!" I exclaim in sheer disbelief.

He turns to me, his jaw dropping open. "Wow, that's definitely not up to code!"

The electric cables form a complex web of crisscrossed chaos; unlike any I have ever seen before. It leaves me wondering how this city has evolved to this point, and the tangled mess stands as a testament to the growth and demand of this city.

It was beautiful and overwhelming all at once. As he drove us to the hotel, the sensory overload deepened. Market stalls spilled into the street, women sold fruit in baskets, meat hung in open air, and children weaved through the crowds. At every turn, there was something new to see. Ornate pagodas and ancient palaces stand alongside contemporary buildings, creating a surreal visual tapestry that tells the story of a city steeped in history yet embracing the future. The traffic is pure chaos, with buses, cars, motorcycles, bicycles, and pedestrians converging on the roads. It appears that traffic rules as we know them in the USA are a mere suggestion here; people and cars cross and turn the streets at will. The air is thick with dust, and the unfortunate truth is that cleanliness lacks.

That first night, I stood by the window of our hotel as the city settled into dusk. The outline of the Himalayas stretched across the horizon. Tomorrow, we would begin the trek. But something inside me had already shifted.

I had faced a mountain before, Kilimanjaro. I had looked down from the summit and realized that the climb is never just physical. It's emotional. It's spiritual.

Before my kidney surgery, the thought of death naturally crossed my mind. Surgery always carries risk, and I'd be lying if I said I didn't wonder, *What if?*

There was a moment when I thought, *Maybe I'll see my parents again.* But deep down, I also knew I would be okay. I had peace in my heart, and I held onto that.

The truth is, we can do anything we set our hearts and minds to. Even after loss. Especially after loss. Donating my kidney and conquering these mountains became living proof of that.

We find new meaning not in what we've lost, but in how we choose to live afterward. For me, it meant building a healthy, active life so my children wouldn't have to experience the kind of pain I did as a child. It also meant giving someone else's family a chance to avoid that same heartbreak, if I could help prevent it. That became my *why*, my motivation.

I'm not saying everyone has to donate a kidney or climb a mountain. But I can say with certainty that joy, beauty, purpose, and laughter can exist, even after devastating loss. It's not easy. It takes grit. It takes heart. But healing is possible. And how we choose to move forward is what writes the next chapter of our story.

I didn't climb these mountains to prove I was strong. I climbed them to remind myself that healing is possible.

There's something few people talk about in the world of donation and advocacy. It's something I've carried quietly through much of my journey: the guilt of being healthy.

The guilt of having the strength to summit mountains in honor of others, while knowing that many are still waiting, still suffering, still hoping. I felt it going into surgery, the heavy awareness that I was walking in by choice, while others lay in hospital beds, tethered to dialysis machines, praying for a call that may never come.

I felt it again during recovery, when my body responded with resilience, when I healed quickly and was back on my feet within days. And I feel it every time I reach a summit, breathless with accomplishment, overlooking the beauty below. The thought always returns. *Why me? Why do I get to do this while someone else waits to simply feel well again?*

Part of the reason, I know, lies in how I've chosen to live my life after loss. I've taken care of my body. I've nourished my spirit. I've pursued healing and leaned into purpose. Still, the guilt is real. It's a quiet ache that lingers beneath the gratitude.

I've come to understand that what I'm feeling is called survivor's guilt. And it's okay. It means I'm human.

What's changed is how I carry it. I've learned to reframe the guilt into something more empowering. I remind myself that this life, this health, this strength is a gift. And the best way to honor a gift is to use it.

To speak up. To advocate. To climb the mountain. To give what I can, while I can.

My strength isn't something I hoard. It's something I offer to the world.

So, if you've ever felt that kind of guilt, whether you're a donor, a survivor, or simply someone who's come through pain while others still struggle, please know you're not alone. Feel it. Acknowledge it, and then, when you're ready, let it go. Because the world doesn't need you to carry guilt, it needs you to keep going, to keep showing up, to keep being the light that others are still reaching for.

The weeklong ascent and descent to Everest Base Camp was one of the most breathtaking and humbling experiences of my life. Each day, we walked for hours, surrounded by towering peaks and prayer flags fluttering in the wind. We crossed suspension bridges strung high above rushing rivers, many adorned with colorful flags and lined with yak trains and fellow trekkers. Along the way, we passed spinning prayer wheels and sacred stone monuments built to honor the mountains and the souls who had come before us.

There was a stillness in the air that grounded me, despite the physical exhaustion. I felt deeply present and vividly alive. Walking that path, a path few in the world will ever take, reminded me how vast and beautiful this planet is, and how fortunate I am to have a body strong enough to carry me there.

But with the beauty came challenges. The high suspension bridges, especially those swaying in the wind, were terrifying. I gripped the sides tightly, willing myself to breathe, my heart pounding with each careful step. Yet with every crossing, I grew braver, surer of myself. I felt the sacred energy of the land move through me.

At night, we stayed in humble tea houses. Warmth didn't come from hot showers, we didn't have those all week, but from shared meals, tired laughter, and the quiet camaraderie of fellow trekkers gathered in rooms heated by fires fueled with yak dung. The Khumbu cough found many of us a dry, persistent irritation brought on by the cold, thin air. Still, even discomfort held its own kind of beauty.

Then came the moment I will never forget: seeing the summit of Everest with my own two eyes. The highest point on Earth, rising before me. It was surreal, sacred, and deeply emotional. A dream I never imagined I would live. One that might never have happened if life had taken another path. But it did happen, because I said yes. Because I kept going.

A few months before the trip, I received a heartfelt request from Claudio, Irving's best friend from medical school. Claudio had lost his wife, Kim, in a tragic accident. Knowing about my upcoming journey, he asked if he and his son could write a letter to her, and if I would carry it with me and read it once I reached Everest Base Camp.

"You'll be closer to heaven than I'll ever be while alive," he told me. "Say hi to Kim for us."

I was deeply moved. I carried that letter close to my heart throughout the entire climb. When we finally reached base camp, I stepped off the trail and found a quiet spot. I read the letter aloud into the cold, thin air, gently tucked it under a rock, and whispered Kim's name in prayer. It was a beautiful, emotional moment. One that reminded me of the sacredness of this journey, and the honor it was to carry someone's love and memory to the top of the world.

Life, like a mountain, is a journey made of steps, some small, some steep, some that feel impossible. But each one carries us closer to where we're meant to be. On the trail to Everest Base Camp, this truth became clear with every hour we hiked. The Base Camp wasn't reached in a single day; it was earned in each deliberate step, each breath taken in the thin mountain air. Life works the same way. Every decision, every act of kindness, every challenge faced becomes part of the climb. And eventually, when we look back, we see just how far we've come.

New opportunities to help others often arise from the most unexpected places. I've come to believe that God's plan for our lives is far greater than anything we could imagine for ourselves. Sometimes, it unfolds slowly, step by step, like a path on the mountain. Other times, it arrives in a flash: a conversation, a stranger's request, or a quiet moment of clarity that whispers, *this is why.*

From admiring El Ávila as a little girl, standing on tiptoes and dreaming of distant peaks, to standing face-to-face with Everest, I've come to see how every chapter of my story has shaped who I am and led me to where I'm meant to be. The path hasn't always made sense, and it was certainly not without pain. But nothing was wasted. Every detour, every loss, and every moment of doubt was preparing me for something greater.

So, I keep going. I keep climbing. I keep showing up for others and for myself, trusting that each small act of kindness and each step taken in faith is part of something far bigger than I may ever fully understand.

Just as Aesop once said, "No act of kindness, no matter how small, is ever wasted."

Figure 62: Kilimanjaro summit

Figure 13: Hanging bridges on the way to EBC

Figure 14: Everest Base Camp

Chapter 8

The Healing Connection

"Take care of your body. It's the only place you have to live." ~*Jim Rohn*

It was December 2nd, 2023. I was sitting on the quiet shore of Isla Mujeres, coffee in hand, the ocean breeze brushing against my skin. For the first time in a long while, I felt still. The kind of stillness that feels like peace, like coming home to yourself. I had arrived for a yoga retreat, a full week of movement, breath, healing, and journaling. What I didn't know was just how much this week would feel like stepping into the very life I had always envisioned.

As I looked out at the blue horizon, a lone pelican soared and dove into the water with effortless grace. The sun was just rising. Boats in the distance bobbed gently in the tide. I whispered to myself, "How did I get so lucky?" A single tear rolled down my cheek. That moment held everything I had worked for—the years of grief, the inner work, the mountains climbed and valleys crossed. And here I was, standing inside the dream.

I picked up the phone and left a message for Dany. "I wish you were here," I told him. "It's beautiful. A pelican just caught its breakfast. The boats are out. I'll call you later. I love you."

Later that morning, our group gathered for yoga on the rooftop. Two rows of ocean-green mats faced the sea. The sun warmed our backs as we moved through breath and flow. Halfway through the practice, I was wrapped in a wave of peace so deep, it felt like a hug from the universe. I realized I was safe. I was steady. I was exactly where I needed to be.

After practice, we shared a nourishing breakfast of papaya, mango, eggs, avocado toast, and green juice. Nothing fancy, but prepared with love and intention. I felt every bite grounding me.

Back in my room, I couldn't stop writing. The thoughts poured out, the way they do when something inside finally clicks into place. I realized I had once believed happiness wasn't meant for me. After losing my dad, my joy had been buried with him. But here, now, surrounded by peace and purpose, I knew that wasn't true. Happiness had simply changed shape.

This moment didn't erase my pain, it honored it. It reminded me that we are shaped by both sorrow and joy, and together they create the mosaic of our lives. That retreat wasn't just a getaway. It was the beginning of something. The moment I finally said, *"This is what I've been working toward."*

Health is the foundation of everything. Without it, even life's simplest joys feel distant. It's not just about avoiding illness or looking a certain way. It's about energy, clarity, resilience, and the ability to show up for the people and moments that matter. Taking care of your health is an act of love for your future self. It means making choices today that support who you want to be tomorrow.

When you nourish your body, move it regularly, and care for your mind and spirit, you build a life that feels good from the inside out. Health isn't a finish line. It's the ground we build everything else upon.

If there's one thing I've learned from walking through the fire of loss, illness, and reinvention, it's this: healing is not a one-time event. It is a lifetime of reconnection to ourselves, to our purpose, to the people we're meant to help, and to the places we're called to explore. Healing is the bridge between your past and your future, between pain and purpose.

If you're at the beginning of your healing, or in the messy middle, please hear this: you are not broken. You are becoming. And the life ahead of you might be more beautiful than you ever imagined.

What I now know is this, healing doesn't always look like green smoothies and yoga poses. Sometimes it looks like giving yourself grace on the hard days. It looks like honoring your story. It looks like listening to your body and trusting that it's been trying to speak to you all along.

As you've read until now, when my dad died, everything changed. Our once vibrant home quickly shifted into survival mode. My mom, grief-stricken and lost, stopped cooking. Family dinners disappeared, along with the structure they once brought. In their place came packaged foods, soda, and processed snacks. I didn't know it then, but that shift in nourishment would echo into my adulthood. We ate to soothe. We chose comfort over nutrition. Though I didn't have the words for it at the time, we were using food to try to fill a hole that food alone could never heal.

I wish I had known then what I know now about the deep connection between food, movement, mindset, and healing. We weren't thinking about health. We were focused on survival. In that space, we forgot to live with purpose. We forgot that our loved ones wouldn't want to see us numb and disconnected. We forgot that life, even after loss, could still be beautiful.

As a radiation therapist and registered nurse, I dedicated my life to caring for others. But it wasn't until adulthood that I began to truly change the way I lived. I was still angry at God for taking my father, for taking my mother too soon, and later, for allowing COVID to tear through our hospitals, our communities, and our profession. In 2022, I left nursing completely burned out. Bitter. Lost. For someone whose identity had been built around helping others, I didn't know who I was anymore.

But sometimes stepping away is what gives us space to find our way back.

At first, walking away from nursing felt like failure. Now, I see it was the opening I needed. It gave me room to breathe. To reflect. To ask, what does healing really look like?

After donating my kidney, I began following the FASTer Way to Fat Loss, a program that helped me track my macros, especially protein. It taught me to see food not as the enemy but as fuel. For the first time, I began to understand my body and its needs. I stopped punishing it. I stopped shaming it. I learned to listen with compassion.

I had already been leaning toward wellness and preventive care, but I still needed guidance. This program helped me rebuild. It gave me back my strength. My confidence. My energy. My joy. Even with one kidney, I felt stronger than I had in years.

The changes came slowly, more energy, fewer crashes, deeper sleep, but something bigger was happening inside me. I was remembering what it felt like to feel whole.

That's what inspired me to become a health coach. I didn't want to keep that knowledge to myself. It felt like a full-circle moment. Everything I'd been through, the losses, the healing, the rebuilding suddenly had purpose.

I turned my focus toward prevention. Toward helping others, especially women navigating midlife and all the chaos it brings. I also began supporting kidney donors like me, guiding them in how to nourish their bodies, trust their strength, and feel safe in their recovery, before and after surgery.

But something was still missing. I had done the physical work. My nutrition was in place, my movement was consistent, and my routines were steady. But my mind was still spinning. That's when I found Emily, my mindset coach, who helped me face the emotional layers I hadn't yet unpacked.

That was also when butterflies began showing up everywhere, in our coaching sessions, in conversations, and even in dreams. I had never liked butterflies, but suddenly, I couldn't ignore them. It was as if the universe was whispering a message: metamorphosis. Transformation. Slowly, I began to see that's what my life had been, a series of cocoons, of breakdowns that led to breakthroughs. I was the caterpillar crawling toward change, and without realizing it, I had been shedding my old self, one painful layer at a time. That transformation spilled over into every part of my life.

This was when the idea to write a book, something that had lived quietly in my heart for years, was reignited. A few years earlier, I had attended a writing retreat at The Watermill in Posara, Italy, led by Jo Parfitt. I had learned how to share life stories with vulnerability and structure. Over time, I had shared parts of my story, on social media, in workshops, through journaling, and with my patients. But now, it was time to tell the whole story. To reflect on the healing journey from grief to purpose, from collapse to reconstruction.

So, I started working with a book coach, and the words began to pour out. The grief. The anger. The resilience. The stories and life lessons. The deep belief that someone, somewhere, needed to know they weren't alone. I allowed myself to believe that my story was worth telling. Not just for me or for my children, but for someone who might see their reflection in it.

Around that same time, Jason, my former massage therapist and friend, reappeared in my life unexpectedly after years of silence. Through social media, I learned that he had lost his son. In the depths of his grief, he found God. His strength and peace amazed me. Week after week, we texted. Sometimes about loss. Sometimes about God. Sometimes just about life. We had moments of disagreement, like old friends often do, but we also laughed and teased each other. He never pushed his beliefs on me. He simply lived them.

And through our conversations, something within me began to stir. I had been away from the Church since Covid, distanced from God by the weight of anger. But without even knowing it, Jason helped reawaken my faith. A spark. A tenderness. A new kind of belief, one no longer rooted in bitterness.

I decided to return to church. I committed to reading the Bible chronologically from beginning to end. I truly believe that every person crosses our path for a reason, arriving at exactly the time they are meant to. Jason's reappearance in my life was proof of that.

Almost as if by divine choreography, I returned to nursing around the same time. It felt like coming full circle. I was offered the perfect oncology nursing job part-time, close to home, and flexible enough to honor my family visits to Italy and my kidney donor treks. It felt like coming home.

In this role, I walk alongside patients from the moment of diagnosis. I help them understand their treatment plans, coordinate appointments, and serve as a bridge between specialties. But more than anything, I help them feel seen.

Cancer is overwhelming. I know that better than most. There's fear, confusion, and a flood of unknowns. Many of the patients I support are newly diagnosed with breast cancer, suddenly thrust into a world they never expected to navigate. I advocate for them. I educate them before surgery, after surgery, and through every uncertain step in between.

I work in the clinic three days a week, supporting two surgeons and a nurse practitioner. The work is challenging, but it's also deeply meaningful. I see the impact every single day.

What a profound honor it has been to end my career in the most meaningful of ways. My past didn't break me, it prepared me. Today, I can sit with patients in their darkest moments and offer knowledge wrapped in compassion. I can hold space for grief without being consumed by it. I teach from lived experience, care with wisdom, and advocate from the heart.

I remind my clients and patients that their body is the only home they'll ever have. I say, *"Feed it with love. Move it with joy. Rest it with intention. And more importantly, forgive it for the years you neglected it. Not because you didn't care, but because you didn't know better. Now you do."*

Healing is not a finish line. It's a thread that weaves together our past, our present, and our potential. Our bodies carry our stories, and when we learn to listen, they lead us home.

If you're on your own healing journey, unsure, overwhelmed, know that you are not alone. There is always a way forward. You don't need to climb a mountain or donate a kidney to find your purpose. You only need to take the next right step. That step might change everything.

I know there are days when getting out of bed feels like climbing Everest. Days when you're lost in fog, uncertain of your next thought, your next breath. I've had those days too. When you can't pull yourself out, start small. Start with nourishment. Just a bite of something that fuels instead of numbs. Because food is more than fuel, it's information. It tells your body how to function, how to feel, and how to heal. But for so many of us, we've been feeding ourselves things that silence the pain while dimming our inner light.

After facing my own health challenges, I began to understand how powerful nutrition truly is. It's not about restriction, it's about respect. When I started treating my body like something I loved, instead of something I needed to fix, everything shifted. Slowly, I began to feel like myself again not just physically, but emotionally and spiritually.

Movement has also been one of the greatest gifts in my healing. Exercise, especially strength training and yoga, reminded me what it feels like to take up space. To stand tall. To feel powerful in my own skin. And on days when I was too exhausted to push, a gentle walk in the sun was enough. Nature became my sanctuary. It doesn't matter how fast you go; it matters that you go. Movement doesn't just reshape your body. It transforms your brain. It shifts your mindset. It builds resilience. It pulls you out of your head and back into your body. For those of us who have lived in survival mode, reconnecting with the body can be revolutionary.

And then there is mindset, the invisible thread that ties it all together. You can eat well and move every day, but if the voice in your head still speaks in shame, doubt, or fear, you won't feel whole. Working with a mindset coach helped me recognize the stories I was still carrying. Stories I never questioned. Stories like, *"I'm not strong enough," "Why did this happen to me?" or "I can't."* Healing asks us to rewrite these narratives. To speak to ourselves with tenderness. To catch the lies and replace them with truth. Every time you speak kindly to yourself, you plant a seed. And over time, those seeds bloom into belief.

Healing rarely happens in isolation. We are wired for connection, yet when we're hurting, we often retreat. We convince ourselves that no one else could possibly understand. But someone out there feels exactly what you feel and they need your story just as much as you need to tell it. Community has been one of the most powerful healing forces in my life. Whether through a fitness group, a support circle, a yoga retreat, or simply a friend who listens without judgment. You need people. Not perfect people, just real ones. The kind who reminds you that progress isn't linear. That healing doesn't mean the sadness disappears. It means you're no longer facing it alone.

It is never too late to rise again. If you're reading this, maybe this is your reminder.

"Start where you are. Use what you have. Do what you can." ~**Arthur Ashe**

Chapter 9

How Would They Want Me to Live?

"Healing is a journey. It is not a linear process, but rather a series of paths, some winding, some steep, and others beautifully unexpected." ~**Mary-Frances Winters**

Healing is a journey marked by switchbacks and unexpected detours. It can feel confusing, exhausting, even disheartening, but it can also be a time of profound transformation, deep emotional growth, and meaningful forward movement. When we begin climbing out of grief, trauma, or long seasons of disconnect, it's easy to become discouraged when the path doesn't look the way we expected. But healing is rarely linear. It loops, pauses, and surprises us. Sometimes we stumble. Sometimes we rise. The most important thing is that we keep going. Every small, uncertain step forward has the potential to shape us into someone wiser, stronger, and more open than we ever thought possible a beautiful butterfly in the making.

We often imagine healing as a staircase, a steady, upward climb. But more often, it's like hiking a mountain in dense fog. You move forward by faith alone. You lose your footing, retrace your steps, and feel like you're going in circles. Then, in a brief moment of clarity, the fog lifts, and you finally see how far you've come.

Grief has a way of shaking our foundation. It disrupts our routines, strains our health, and alters our ability to care for ourselves. It tempts us to retreat into old patterns, to numb the pain with unhealthy habits. But there is a gentler, more life-giving way forward.

This six-week guide is designed to support your whole self, body, mind, and spirit, as you walk through the tender landscape of loss. It is not a quick fix. Instead, it offers steady companionship as you rebuild, realign, and rediscover your strength one intentional step at a time.

Throughout these six weeks, I encourage you to care deeply for yourself and to let others care for you too. Accept the home-cooked meal. Say yes to the walk with a friend. Let kind words in. Grief may feel isolating, but healing happens in connection. You are not meant to walk this path alone.

Many of the practices I share are drawn from my own journey of healing. They are offered with compassion, not as prescriptions. There is no single right way to grieve. Each person's experience is as unique as their loss. What brings comfort to one may not resonate with another and that's okay. The most important thing is to keep moving gently forward, honoring your emotions, and discovering what feels healing and true for you.

This six-week journey into healing is designed to meet you exactly where you are with grace, not pressure. Each week offers prompts for Monday through Friday, giving you space to reflect, reset, and reconnect over the weekend. You might choose to revisit a prompt, spend time outdoors, attend church, journal in silence, or simply rest. The weekends are yours to breathe and just be.

Healing is not a checklist to race through. It's about allowing space for your soul to catch up. Give yourself permission to slow down. Let what you're discovering settle deeply. Honor the rhythm that feels true to you before stepping into a new week.

Most importantly, remember this: simply living your life as your loved one would have wanted is enough. Healing does not mean forgetting. It means carrying their memory forward with love and purpose as you begin again.

I hope to be remembered as someone who used her voice, her story, and her journey to help others rise. I want to leave behind a trail of kindness, healing, and strength, a reminder that even after great loss, you can rebuild a life that is meaningful, beautiful, and whole.

Know that I feel you. I see you. I hear you. And I want to encourage you to care for your body, mind, and spirit in the sacred aftermath of loss. May the ripple effect of my life inspire you to live with intention, to keep going, and to trust that something greater exists beyond the pain you've endured.

Week 1: Prep Week – Laying the Foundation
Monday: Honor Your Body

Your body is remarkable, and it deserves care and respect. Grief can take a toll physically, but by focusing on small, nurturing habits, you can start the healing process.

Reflection: What actions can you take this week to honor your body during this challenging time? Write them below.

Here are some examples of actions you can take this week to honor your body during a challenging time:

1. Commit to drinking enough water daily to stay hydrated and support your body's needs.

2. Choose gentle movement like walking, yoga, or stretching to release tension and support circulation.

3. Nourish yourself with balanced meals, focusing on whole, nutrient-dense foods that fuel your energy.

4. Prioritize rest by setting a consistent bedtime and creating a calming nighttime routine.

5. Practice deep breathing or meditation to reduce stress and reconnect with your body.

6. Spend a few moments outdoors to soak in natural light and boost your mood.

7. Treat yourself to a massage to ease physical tension.

8. Allow yourself permission to rest and take breaks as needed without guilt.

_____

_____

_____

Tuesday: Letting Go

Fasting, whether it's from certain foods, behaviors, or distractions, can be a powerful tool for clearing space in your life. What can you let go of to create room for healing?

Reflection: What physical or emotional burden can you release today to allow more space for your wellness?

Examples could be:

1.   Consider releasing clutter in your physical space by organizing a drawer, closet, or room. Letting go of excess can create a sense of calm and clarity.

2.   Let go of self-criticism or guilt by practicing self-compassion. Write down one negative thought you've been holding onto and reframe it with kindness toward yourself.

_____

_____

_____

Wednesday: Nourish from Within

Whole, nourishing foods help fuel your body and your mind. Focus on what you can introduce to your meals that will truly nourish you from the inside out.

Reflection: What whole foods can you add to your diet this week to support your healing?

You could try:

1. Adding fresh vegetables like spinach to smoothies, salads, or soups to boost nutrients like iron, calcium, and vitamins.

2. Incorporate foods like avocados, nuts, or seeds into your diet to support brain health and reduce inflammation during your healing process.

Thursday: Shift Your Perspective

Grief can cloud your thinking, but small shifts in your perspective can have a big impact. Focus on growth, healing, and self-compassion this week.

Reflection: What mindset shift can you focus on this week to support your emotional well-being?

Some examples might be:

Negative Thought: "I'll never feel like myself again."

Positive Reframe: "Healing takes time, but each day brings me closer to discovering a new version of myself."

Negative Thought: "I'm failing at coping with this."

Positive Reframe: "I'm doing my best, and it's okay to ask for help when I need it. Healing takes time."

Friday: Acknowledge Your Progress

Every small step toward wellness is worth celebrating. Reflect on the progress you've made this week and recognize how far you've come.

Reflection: What progress, no matter how small, can you celebrate today?

Here are some things to be celebrated:

1. **Getting Out of Bed:** Acknowledging the effort it took to start the day despite the weight of grief.

2. **Reaching Out:** Calling or texting a loved one for support or connection.

3. **Completing a Task:** Finishing even a small chore like doing the dishes or folding laundry.

4. **Eating a Balanced Meal:** Taking time to nourish your body with healthy food.

5. **Practicing Self-Care:** Engaging in an activity like taking a walk, journaling, or meditating.

6. **Allowing Emotions:** Giving yourself permission to cry, feel, or simply rest without judgment.

7. **Reflecting on Good Memories:** Smiling or laughing at a cherished memory of your loved one.

_____

_____

_____

_____

Week 2: Balanced Nutrition – Fueling Your Body and Soul

Monday: Respect Your Body

Balanced nutrition is a key part of respecting your body's needs during grief. Focus on including proteins, healthy fats, and carbohydrates in the right amounts to fuel your body.

Reflection: How can you make small improvements to your nutrition this week? What nutrients can you focus on? Try something new.

1. **Incorporate More Protein:** Add a new source of lean protein, such as lentils or grilled fish, to your meals this week to support muscle repair and energy.

2. **Try a New Vegetable:** Experiment with a nutrient-rich vegetable you haven't had before, like roasted brussels sprouts or sautéed bok choy, to add variety and vitamins to your diet.

Tuesday: Consistency Matters

Consistency in your eating habits can be challenging during grief, but even small, balanced meals can make a huge difference.

Reflection: What is one thing you can do consistently this week to nourish your body?

Some examples might be:

1. **Move Your Body:** Commit to a daily walk to keep your body active.

2. **Focus on Protein:** Include a source of protein in each meal to fuel and repair your body.

3. **Mindful Eating:** Eat slowly and focus on enjoying each bite without distractions.

4. **Try a Smoothie:** Make a nutrient-packed smoothie with fruits, greens, and healthy fats for a quick and nourishing option.

_____

_____

_____

Wednesday: Mindful Eating

Pay attention to how you feel before, during, and after eating. Eating mindfully allows you to tune into your body's real needs. Even if you are not hungry, try to eat.

Reflection: How can mindful eating help you better connect with your body's needs? What does your body need today?

An example might be, while eating breakfast mindfully, you notice you're drawn to warm, comforting foods, suggesting your body might need grounding nourishment. A bowl of oatmeal topped with nuts and berries provides the balance your body craves today.

Thursday: Rebalance

Grief can cause us to crave comfort foods, but focusing on rebalancing your meals can help stabilize both your energy and emotions.

Reflection: How can you rebalance your meals this week to support both your physical and emotional well-being?

This week, you could focus on rebalancing your meals by adding a mix of protein, healthy fats, and fiber-rich carbohydrates to each plate. For instance, pair grilled chicken (protein) with avocado slices (healthy fats) and brown rice or roasted sweet potatoes (fiber-rich carbs). This balance can help stabilize your blood sugar, boost your mood, and provide steady energy throughout the day.

Friday: Celebrate Balance

Achieving balance in your nutrition is a victory. Reflect on how your nutritional changes have impacted your energy, mood, and overall wellness.

Reflection: What positive effects have you noticed from eating more balanced meals this week?

This could be an example:

"Eating more balanced meals this week has helped me feel more grounded and emotionally steady. By nourishing my body with whole foods, I've noticed it's easier to manage overwhelming emotions and find moments of clarity, giving me the strength to slowly heal."

Week 3: Movement – Releasing Grief through Physical Activity

Monday: Care Through Movement

Movement can help release the tension and emotions stored in your body. Even gentle movement can have a powerful impact on your physical and emotional health.

Reflection: How can you incorporate movement into your routine this week? What feels most manageable right now?

1. **Gentle Walks in Nature:** Taking a 10–15-minute walk outside, even if just around your neighborhood, can help you reconnect with the world around you. Walking allows your body to release tension and stress hormones, promotes blood flow, and provides a change of scenery, which can be uplifting when you're feeling stuck in grief. It's a small step that helps ground you in the present moment.

2. **Simple Yoga or Stretching:** Starting your day with a few gentle yoga poses or stretches, like child's pose or downward dog, can help loosen physical

tightness often caused by grief. Movement encourages the release of endorphins, which can improve mood and provide a sense of relief.

Tuesday: Small Steps Forward

Start small. Whether it's stretching, walking, or yoga, find a way to move your body that feels supportive, not overwhelming.

Reflection: What small movement can you commit to today? How does it make you feel afterward?

Not all days will feel the same, some days will be harder than others.

1. **Stretching for Five Minutes:** Commit to a simple five-minute stretch routine in the morning. Stretching helps release tension in your body, improves circulation, and creates a sense of calm.

Afterward, you might feel more relaxed and grounded, ready to take on the day.

2. Walking Around the House or Yard: If stepping outside feels like too much, commit to walking around your home or yard for a few minutes. Movement, no matter how small, can lift your mood, ease feelings of stagnation, and remind you that you're capable of taking steps forward, both physically and emotionally.

_____

_____

_____

Wednesday: Mind-Body Connection

Physical activity can help you reconnect with your body. Use movement as a way to become more present in your healing journey.

Reflection: How does moving your body change the way you feel emotionally? What is your body asking for today?

Movement has a profound effect on emotions because it encourages the release of endorphins, the body's natural "feel-good" chemicals. It also shifts your focus away from intrusive thoughts and helps anchor you in the present moment. Movement can also create a sense of accomplishment, no matter how small, which boosts self-confidence and reinforces resilience in your healing journey. You could try joining a class or a group, if you feel this is appropriate at this time.

Thursday: Strength in Motion

Strength comes in many forms. As you move through grief, allow physical activity to remind you of your inner strength and resilience.

Reflection: How can you build strength through movement? What type of physical activity feels most empowering?

Incorporating light weights or bodyweight exercises like squats or push-ups can remind you of your physical capabilities. As you gradually build muscle and endurance, you may also feel a boost in confidence and empowerment, reinforcing the strength you carry internally. You can do this!

_____

_____

_____

Friday: Celebrate Movement

Every time you move your body, you're contributing to your healing. Celebrate the physical and emotional benefits of the movement you've embraced this week.

Reflection: What have you noticed about how movement has impacted your mood and energy this week? Journaling is very important.

For example, "This week, I noticed that even a short walk outside lifted my mood. Moving my body gave me a sense of accomplishment, even on difficult days, and helped me feel more connected to myself."

Or, "Stretching each morning gave me a small energy boost that carried me through the day. I've felt less sluggish and more motivated to face the tasks ahead, even when grief feels heavy."

Week 4: Emotional Detox – Releasing Grief in Healthy Ways

Monday: Clear Your Mind

Sometimes, we need to detox emotionally. Take time today to clear your mind, whether through journaling, meditation, or simply sitting in stillness.

Reflection: What are you holding onto? How can you start letting go today?

Try doing a 5 or 10 minute "brain dump" you could expand on something like this "I've been holding onto feelings of guilt about not being as productive as I used to be. Today, I can start letting go by journaling my thoughts and reminding myself that healing takes time, and it's okay to rest."

Get a nice journal and use it daily, either first thing in the morning, during the day as needed or before bed.

_____

_____

_____

Tuesday: Release and Renew

Grief can build up like toxins in the body. Find a way today to release some of the weight you've been carrying, whether through talking, writing, or moving.

Reflection: How do you feel when you allow yourself to release emotions?

An example besides journaling can be:

Call a Friend: "I called a close friend today to share how I've been feeling. Talking to someone who listens without judgment helped me feel less alone. Afterward, I went for a walk outside and focused on my breath."

Wednesday: Self-Care is Essential

Self-care isn't just a buzzword; it's essential for healing. Take time today to do something purely for yourself, even if it's something small.

Reflection: What self-care practice can you prioritize today? How does it make you feel afterward?

Some examples could be:

1. **Taking a Warm Bath:** "I soaked in a warm bath with calming scents like lavender. It helped me relax, release tension. Afterward, I felt calmer."

2. **Reading a Book:** "I spent 30 minutes reading a book that I enjoy. Focusing on the story helped me escape from my worries for a while, and afterward, I felt more centered."

See the list of books in chapter 4, pick one and begin.

Thursday: Detox from Negativity

Grief can often bring negative thoughts or feelings. Today, focus on detoxing from negativity by intentionally replacing those thoughts with something kind or hopeful.

Reflection: What negative thoughts can you release today? What positive, hopeful idea can you replace it with?

- **Negative Thought:** "I'll never feel like myself again."

- **Positive, Hopeful Idea:** "Healing takes time, but each day I am growing stronger and discovering a new version of myself that is capable and resilient."

Replacing negative thoughts with hopeful ideas helps create a mindset shift that supports healing.

Friday: Celebrate Your Emotional Strength

You've worked hard this week to release, renew, and care for yourself. Acknowledge the emotional strength you've built through this process.

Reflection: What emotional progress have you made this week? How has it impacted your overall sense of well-being? Remember grief is not linear, and it doesn't have to look like progress.

For example, "This week, I allowed myself to cry when I felt overwhelmed instead of suppressing my emotions. Letting the feelings flow without judgment has helped me release some of the heaviness I've been carrying."

Week 5: Mindset – Shifting Thoughts to Support Healing

Monday: Nurture Your Body and Mind

Your mindset impacts how you care for both your body and mind. This week, focus on nurturing yourself through positive thoughts and supportive habits. We have worked on this already a little bit, but it is so important to feel ALL the feelings and make small mindset shifts when we feel stuck.

Reflection: What mindset shift can help you better support your healing this week?

Examples of Mindset Shifts:

1. **From "I have to do everything" to "I can take it one step at a time":** Shifting your mindset to focus on small, manageable actions instead of feeling overwhelmed by the bigger picture can help you approach healing with patience and self-compassion.

2. **From "Healing should be fast" to "Healing is a journey":** Reminding yourself that healing is not linear and giving yourself grace through ups and downs can alleviate frustration.

3. **From "I'm stuck in my pain" to "I'm growing through my pain":** Reframing grief as an opportunity for growth can help you see the strength you're building and the ways you're learning to navigate challenges.

4. **From "I'm alone in this" to "I can lean on others":** Allowing yourself to seek support from loved ones, friends, or a community can remind you that you don't have to carry the weight of healing by yourself.

_____

_____

_____

Tuesday: Clear Your Mental Space

Fasting from negative thoughts or distractions can help clear mental clutter. Use this time to create space for new, healthier thoughts to take root.

Reflection: What can you let go of mentally to create more clarity and focus?

An example might be:

Overthinking the Future: "I can release the habit of overthinking what's ahead and focus on the present moment instead. Trusting that each step I take is enough can help me feel more clear-headed. I take one day at a time, one hour at a time."

I know we've talked a lot about the mind, but this is the area I struggled with the most. I either did not want to think about it at all, wishing I had amnesia, or when I did, I did not know what to do with my thoughts.

Wednesday: Reframe Challenges

Grief brings challenges, but shifting your perspective can help you reframe these obstacles as opportunities for growth.

Reflection: What challenge are you facing right now that you can reframe? How can you view it as an opportunity for growth?

Examples of Reframing Challenges:

1. **School Stress:** *Challenge:* "Balancing grief with the demands of school feels overwhelming." *Reframe:* "This challenge is teaching me time management and resilience. By tackling one assignment at a time, I'm proving to myself that I can keep moving forward, even during difficult times."

2. **Holiday Gatherings:** *Challenge:* "Facing the holidays without a loved one feels heartbreaking and I don't want to celebrate." *Reframe:* "While it's painful, this is an opportunity to honor their memory by creating new traditions or sharing stories about them, keeping their spirit alive in meaningful ways."

3. **Managing Home Responsibilities:** *Challenge:* "Keeping up with daily tasks at home feels exhausting."

Reframe: "This is teaching me the importance of asking for help, learning new skills and setting boundaries."

_____

_____

_____

Thursday: Build Resilience

Resilience is built through small, consistent shifts. Focus on how you can build emotional strength through each of your daily choices.

Reflection: How can you build resilience today? What small step can you take toward strengthening your body and mindset?

Examples for Building Resilience:

1. **Practice Gratitude:** *Action:* "Today, I will write down three things I'm grateful for, even small ones like a kind word or a good meal." Focusing on gratitude shifts your mindset from loss to appreciation, helping you see the positives even in challenging times.

2. **Set a Simple Goal:** *Action:* "I will clean one small space, like my desk, to feel more organized and in control." Taking action toward achievable goals

reminds you that progress is possible, even in the midst of grief, and strengthens your confidence.

Friday: Celebrate Your Mindset Shifts

Celebrate the mindset shifts you've made this week. Acknowledge how these changes are helping you heal, and continue moving forward.

Reflection: What mindset shifts have had the biggest impact on you? How do they help you feel more in control of your healing?

Mindset Shift Example: *"I've started viewing setbacks not as failures but as opportunities to learn and grow."* This shift has helped you release self-judgment and approach challenges with hope instead of frustration. It's made you more patient with yourself and given you confidence in your ability to move forward, even on difficult days. This new perspective reminds you that healing is a process, and progress no matter how small is worth celebrating.

Week 6: Support – Finding Strength in Community

Monday: Connection is Key

Healing doesn't happen in isolation. Reach out to others, whether friends, family, or support groups, who can walk this journey with you.

Reflection: How can connecting with others support your healing journey? Who can you reach out to for support?

Examples of Connection for Healing:

1. **Join a Support Group:** Many hospitals or community centers offer grief or loss support groups. Joining one can help you connect with others who truly understand your experience. Hearing their stories and sharing your own can reduce feelings of isolation.

2. **Reach Out to Someone with a Similar Experience:** If you know someone who has gone through a similar loss, consider reaching out. They may offer unique insights or simply lend a compassionate ear, reminding you that you're not alone in your journey.

3. **Lean on Family or Friends:** Reaching out to a trusted family member or friend can provide comfort. Letting them know you need their support, even for something as simple as sitting together in silence.

_____

_____

_____

Tuesday: Shared Strength

When you share your struggles, you gain strength from others. Be open to sharing and receiving support, it can make all the difference in your healing. We might believe no one can truly understand the pain we are going through, and although there is some truth to that, you might also realize others who have been through something similar can be a great source of strength for you.

Reflection: How can sharing your experience with others help you heal? What strength can you offer to someone else?

Examples of Sharing and Receiving Strength:

1. **Sharing Your Story in a Support Group:** *Reflection:* "By sharing my experience in a grief support group, I realized I'm not alone in my pain. Hearing others' stories reminded me that healing is possible, and my story might help someone else too."

2. **Offering Encouragement to a Friend:** *Reflection:* "I reached out to a friend who recently experienced a loss and shared how I've been coping.

Offering them words of encouragement helped me feel a sense of purpose."

_____

_____

_____

Wednesday: Support Through Nourishment

Sometimes, support comes in the form of nourishment, whether it's a meal prepared by a friend or simply time spent with loved ones.

Reflection: How can you nourish both your body and your relationships this week? What does community care look like for you?

Examples of Support

1. **Accepting Help from Others:** "This week, I'll allow a friend to bring over a meal they offered to prepare. Accepting their care reminds me that I'm not alone and that community support can come in many forms. It helps me focus on healing while feeling cared for by those around me."

2. **Spending Quality Time:** "I'll schedule a coffee date with a friend to catch up and share how we're both doing. This time together will nourish my relationships and remind me of the importance of connection as part of my healing journey."

Thursday: Strength in Numbers

A community can help you shift your mindset and provide encouragement when you feel stuck. Surround yourself with those who understand your journey.

Reflection: How has the community helped you navigate your grief? What have you learned from others along the way? "Being part of a support group at the local hospital has been invaluable. Listening to others who have experienced similar losses helps me feel less alone. Their stories remind me that my emotions are valid and that healing takes time. Community has provided a safe space to share my pain without judgment."

_____

_____

_____

Friday: Celebrate Your Support System

Celebrate the strength you've gained from your community and the support system you've built. Healing is a collective effort, and you're not alone.

Reflection: How has your support system helped you heal? What connections are you most grateful for today?

"My support system has given me a safe place to express my feelings without fear of judgment. Whether it's a trusted friend, family member, or a group I joined, their listening ears and understanding have reminded me that I don't have to navigate this journey alone."

"I'm deeply grateful for friends and family who made the effort to check in, even when I didn't ask. Whether it was through a message or simply sitting with me in silence, their kindness showed me the power of genuine connection."

Healing is never a solitary journey; it's a collective effort made possible by the people who lift you up along the way. It reminds you that, while grief is a heavy load, it's shared across many shoulders, making it a little lighter to carry.

As you reach the end of this final chapter, I hope you feel seen. Grief has a way of breaking everything open, making the world feel unfamiliar and even your own reflection hard to recognize. It's easy to fall into an "all or nothing" mindset, to believe that if we can't feel whole, we shouldn't even try. But healing isn't about perfection. It's about presence.

This six-week grief and wellness guide was never meant to fix your pain. It was created to gently lead you back to yourself, one small and compassionate habit at a time.

You may not feel ready to leap into joy or embrace purpose just yet and that is perfectly okay. But with each mindful choice, each act of care, you will begin to notice something: life still holds meaning. Not in spite of your grief, but because of the depth of your love.

These simple daily practices are here to help you rediscover your rhythm, reconnect with your body and spirit, and begin, little by little, to shape a life that feels whole again. You are not alone. You are not broken. You are becoming one breath, one habit, one day at a time.

Conclusion

There comes a moment in every journey when you realize the end isn't really an end at all. It's a beginning. Writing this book and living this book has shown me that healing is not about returning to who we were before the pain. It's about becoming someone deeper, softer, braver, and more awake because of it.

I didn't set out to live this story. I didn't ask to lose my father so young, to walk through the grief of my mother's passing, or to endure the unraveling of identity that often follows trauma. I never expected to change careers more than once, to donate a kidney, or to summit mountains.

But life, in its mysterious and often messy way, had other plans. And somewhere along that path, I began to see the thread, the purpose, the meaning, and the unexpected beauty.

This memoir is more than a collection of memories. It is a tribute to the quiet transformation that happens when we choose to keep going, even when everything inside us wants to stop. It is a reminder that healing doesn't come in one grand, sweeping moment. It comes in the small, everyday choices to nourish our bodies, challenge our minds, nurture our spirits, and open our hearts.

I've learned that we don't heal by pretending everything is fine. We heal by telling the truth—first to ourselves, then to others. We heal by showing up, cracked and uncertain, and allowing the light to seep through the broken places. We heal through community, through connection, and through finding purpose again. And we heal by choosing to see the gift in every season, even the ones we never asked for.

If there's one message, I want to leave you with, it's this: **You are not alone**. No matter where you are in your journey, whether you're taking your first step, feeling lost in the middle, or catching your breath at the summit, you belong here. You are worthy of healing. You are capable of joy. And it is not too late for you.

My story isn't over. Neither is yours. So, let's keep writing. Let's keep rising. Let's keep becoming who we were always meant to be, not just caterpillars, but butterflies in full flight.

This is metamorphosis: the gift of a life lived twice. A life before loss, and a life after. A life grounded in struggle, and lifted by transformation.

May my story and the lessons I've gathered help you believe that your life can still be filled with meaning and purpose after loss. It will not be easy. But it is possible.

Do it for yourself. Do it for your family. Do it for the one you lost.

Acknowledgments

Writing this memoir has been a journey of the heart, and I could never have done it alone. These pages hold the lessons I've learned from every writer I've read, every teacher who guided me, every patient, client, colleague, friend, and family member who shared space, stories, and strength with me. You inspired these words more than you know.

To my family, I begin with my parents, Pier Franco and Diana Fontana, my sister Margherita Fontana, my husband Daniel Gomes, and most of all, my children, Gabriela, Tomás, and Alex Gomes, who always encouraged me to share my story. Your love gave me the courage to write freely and openly, with the hope that my words might help and inspire others.

To my Italian family, too many to name, but especially my great-grandmother Ermelinda Fontana, my grandparents Edoardo and Caterina Fontana, my great-aunt Bellarmina Fontana, Giulio and Fernanda Berti, Nicla and Mario Porta, Letizia and Marcella Berti, Francesco Porta, and Giovanna

Porta. Thank you for inspiring me and loving me through some of the hardest moments of my life.

To my high school friends, Ana María Fernandez, Patricia Cuadra, Claudia Di Rienzo, Alexandra Gonzalez, Deborah Binchi, Carolina Aquique, Silvia Neresoff, and many others. To my Italian friends, Valeria Venturini, Stefania DiMasso, Paola Pasquini, Andrea Tagliaferro, Laura Tagliaferro, Aldo and Lucia Corrini. And to my college friends, Josmar Fuenmayor, María Belen Fuentes, Irving Marquez, Claudio Faenza, Andrés Guelrud, and Elizabeth Garami. Your support and friendship brought me comfort, laughter, and strength in moments of doubt.

To Jo Parfitt and the wonderful team at The Watermill at Posara, including Lois and Bill Breckon. Thank you for nurturing my writing voice and helping me believe I had something meaningful to share.

To Sandra Rodriguez Bicknell, my book coach, thank you for giving me the blueprint and confidence to begin, even before I felt ready.

To Emily Judice, my mindset coach, thank you for walking beside me through the messy middle. Your presence and insight helped me release old stories and uncover my truth.

To Dr. John Powelson, my kidney surgeon, mentor, and friend. Thank you for helping me turn a life-changing decision into a lifelong mission of love and purpose.

To my fellow kidney donor trekkers, Bobby McLaughlin, Giannon Goldhagen, Jessica Kenaston, and Kenny Neher. Thank you for being part of this incredible mountain journey. I hope we continue climbing together for years to come.

To Embark Exploration, especially Carrie O'Callaghan and Donovan Patcholl. Thank you for designing treks that have made raising awareness about kidney donation a breathtaking and meaningful experience.

To The Faster Way to Fat Loss. Thank you for transforming my health and preparing me to become a coach, allowing me to empower countless women to do the same.

To my editors, my cover designer, and the entire team at Soulfully Aligned Publishing. Thank you for your thoughtful care in shaping this book and for capturing the essence of my story with such beauty and intention.

And to my readers. Thank you for welcoming me into your hearts, for walking this journey alongside me, for seeing pieces of your own story in mine, and for letting these words meet you where you are. It is one of the greatest honors of my life to share this with you.

Thank You

Thank you from the bottom of my heart for reading this book. Whether you found it during a season of grief, sought comfort in shared stories, or simply followed a quiet curiosity, I'm deeply grateful you chose to walk this path with me.

Writing this memoir was an act of courage. It asked me to return to some of the most painful chapters of my life. But in doing so, I rediscovered the quiet strength that comes from honesty, the unexpected beauty within healing, and the profound connection we find in our shared humanity.

The fact that these words have reached your hands means more to me than I can express.

You've now become part of this journey. If something in these pages resonated with you, I'd love to hear about it. Your reflections, your thoughts, and your own story matter to me. Connection doesn't end on the last page.

You can find me online and reach out through:

🌿 Instagram: @criselba.wellness

🌿 Website: www.cristinafontanawellness.com

Email: cris.elba68@gmail.com

If this book touched your heart, please leave a review or share it with a friend who might need it. That simple act helps spread the message of hope and healing to someone else who may be struggling.

Most of all, thank you for being here, for showing up for yourself, and for allowing me to be a small part of your story.

With all my love and gratitude,

Cristina Fontana

Author Bio

CRISTINA FONTANA is proof that life's hardest chapters can become your greatest calling. A registered nurse, oncology nurse navigator, health coach, yoga teacher, and living kidney donor, Cristina blends science and soul to help midlife women and kidney donors transform their health and reclaim their purpose. Her debut memoir, *Metamorphosis: The Gift of a Life Lived Twice*, traces her path through grief, reinvention, and healing—from losing her father at 14 to donating her kidney decades later in his honor.

Cristina has built a diverse and meaningful career across radiation oncology, pediatrics, and transplant coordination. She currently serves as a breast cancer nurse navigator at IU Health's Schwarz Cancer Center, offering compassionate, expert support to patients through some of their most vulnerable moments. In addition to her clinical work, she's a certified FASTer Way health coach, macro nutrition and hormone specialist, 200-hour RYT yoga instructor, and certified yoga4cancer® teacher—bringing a holistic, science-backed approach to wellness.

Her story and expertise have been featured by IU Health, Kidney Donor Athletes, The Indianapolis Star, and Channel 13 News, as well as on wellness podcasts like *Living a Badassery Life*, *Self-Care Level 1000*, and *Something Significant with Matt Gersper*. Cristina's writing also appears in *Stroll Stonegate*, a local magazine in Zionsville, Indiana, where she shares inspiration and practical tools for living with strength and purpose.

She lives in Zionsville with her husband of 30+ years, Daniel, and is a proud mom to three grown children—Gabriela, Tomas, and Alex—and a joyful Nonna to Audrey.

Find her at cristinafontanawellness.com and on Instagram @criselba.wellness.

She believes one act of kindness—like donating a kidney—can change both the recipient and the donor's life, and that it's always worth loving boldly and doing something a little wild.

About The Publisher

Soulfully Aligned Publishing

PUBLISHING

Welcome to Soulfully Aligned Publishing, where we believe that the power of words can transform lives. As the founder and book coach, I am dedicated to guiding you on your path to becoming a published author.

Our mission is to empower and inspire you to share your unique story with the world in a way that is authentic and aligned with your soul's purpose. Whether you are a seasoned writer or just starting out, we provide you with the personalized support and resources you need to bring your vision to life.

Through our coaching, editing, and publishing services, we help you elevate your message and amplify your voice. Let us embark on this transformative journey together.

Explore our website and connect with me, Sandra Rodriguez Bicknell, to discover how we can help you manifest your literary dreams with grace and elegance.

www.sandrarodriguezbicknell.com

www.ingramcontent.com/pod-product-compliance
Lightning Source LLC
Chambersburg PA
CBHW031305120626
46554CB00001BA/283

9 798989 074976